Twelve

12 Life Principles For Your Twenties And Early Thirties

By

Al Golzari

Copyright 2023 by Al Golzari

All Rights Reserved

ISBN-13: 979-8-218-21293-3

GPG, LLC

AVALON GUIDEBOOKS

No part of this book may be reproduced by any mechanical, photographic, or electronic process, or otherwise copied for public or private use—other than for "fair use" as brief quotations embodied in articles and reviews—without prior written permission from the author.

Please consider subscribing to my YouTube channel: Al Golzari. Check out my videos on marketing, presentation skills, business writing, and many more topics.

Also, consider my other books, on presentation skills and business writing skills.

It's Called Presenting, Not Talking Out Loud: A Quick, Strategic Guide For Effective Presentations.

Businesspeople Don't Read, We Scan: A Quick, Strategic Guide For Effective Business Writing.

ACKNOWLEDGMENTS

This book is dedicated to all those in the world who give a damn.

You know who you are. And you know what I mean.

And thank you.

INTRODUCTION: WHY I WROTE THIS BOOK AND HAVE SO MUCH FAITH IN YOU

I'm not here to give you a lecture on why it's good to be young. I'm not here to tell you the good and bad points of young people. I won't lecture you on the importance of being safe when it comes to your personal decisions. Nor am I here to tell you some sappy nonsense that you are the future. I believe in all the above, by the way. But that's not why I wrote this book. <u>You don't need me for that</u>.

I wrote this book because I genuinely care about you. I really do.

What you'll get from me in this book is the straight dope.

You're going to get the good 'medicine' from me. Not the street drugs that are laced with a lot of filler and junk and the stuff that can kill you, literally and figuratively. You're getting the good stuff here. Pharmaceutical, Grade A purity.

And here's what I think...

I think you have the opportunity to do something that most of the world never gets a chance to do:

Change the social narrative.

So many of the things you see around you in your life...you can change them if you want to. Institutions, practices, values, etc. You can. You just need to want it.

And I think what I have to share with you can, and will, help you.

This book, admittedly, was hard for me to write and took longer than anticipated (a lot longer). I went through many chapter edits and deleted certain topics entirely. Sometimes what I had written seemed to be too aligned with what's currently going on. And since I want this book to be as timeless as possible, I've focused here on topics that I think are fundamental.

Another issue that was important to me was to not provide you with advice. In other words, you won't find any, 'Do this' or 'Don't do that' here. This book is strategic in nature and should be seen as a guidebook. Maybe even a handbook.

The topics in this book are essentially what I think are the most important things that you should know. Or, if you know about them, you may not know them to the point where you can really use them to your advantage.

In many ways, the themes in the book have been in my head for over 20 years (evolving, of course) and I never knew how to communicate and share them, aside from a few close friends. But that's not SCALE. I've always wanted scale! Maybe this is a first step to achieving that.

I've always been concerned with the human condition and consider myself a social gadfly, or social instigator, of sorts. In some ways it's fair to say I also play the role of social agitator. Saying lots of things – but always for what I think are the right reasons, to improve people's lives and the belief that people can improve their lives, if they try.

I'm a business guy, but also part sociologist. I never asked for any of this. It just is.

I also have a second career in teaching college, which never came by accident; it was always something I also wanted, by design.

I started a 'Special Lecture' in 2018 in one course where the students were just wonderful, and they all understood me. And started doing this special lecture here and there in various classes, since. And for the most part, students seemed to appreciate what I was sharing. This book, while more exhaustive, was born from the special lectures. Each chapter starts with a point and purpose of what you're about to read, and I hope that will help further its value.

I've also tried my best to not come across as judgmental, except for a few areas where I felt it's justified – and hope I've succeeded. That was important to me. Because I really want you to benefit from this. And I want you to know, in a very sincere way, this book is about you, not me.

You also won't find any bravado here. The only time I'll talk about myself in this book is when I think it's appropriate as an introduction, or some type of backdrop to provide context.

You also won't find advice that I've made 'personal.' Of course, I've provided some of my own experiences and perspectives throughout the book, in a general way. In other words, just because I may have been impacted by something, it doesn't mean you will.

Each topic is presented in a way that is hopefully not only useful, but ACTIONABLE. This book is the culmination of years of my experiences, thoughts, and insights. I hope that you don't just find this 'interesting.' In other words, hopefully you can synthesize this. Actionable nuggets, as I like to call them.

So ultimately, why did I write this book? Because I want to do my small part in helping you become the most productive and successful person you can be, in whatever way you decide to define those terms.

As one of my heroes (and favorite business hero), Steve Jobs, famously said:

*The best way to predict the future...is to **create** it.*

Let's get started...

TABLE OF CONTENTS

CHAPTER ONE | WHAT DO YOU WANT TO DO WITH YOUR LIFE? 17

CHAPTER TWO | SELF-AWARENESS 32

CHAPTER THREE | DEAR BIG MOUTHS (LIKE ME), THIS ONE'S FOR YOU 44

CHAPTER FOUR | OWNERSHIP IS THE WAY TO A FULFILLING LIFE 73

CHAPTER FIVE | EMBRACING STAND-UP COMEDY 87

CHAPTER SIX | MOST THINGS IN LIFE BOIL DOWN TO MONEY 95

CHAPTER SEVEN | RELAX, ALMOST EVERYONE PANDERS TO THEIR BASE 107

CHAPTER EIGHT | POWER, PERSUASION, AND CHANGE 121

CHAPTER NINE | LIKABILITY 133

CHAPTER TEN | CORPORATE CULTURE AND POLITICS 143

CHAPTER ELEVEN | POLITICIANS AND POLITICS 163

CHAPTER TWELVE | NUANCE 175

CONCLUSION 181

BONUS CHAPTER: CHAPTER FIVE FROM MY PRESENTATION SKILLS BOOK 183

BONUS CHAPTER: MOST THINGS ARE AN 'INSIDE JOB' 195

BONUS CHAPTER: HOW TO ADMIRE YOUR HEROES THE RIGHT WAY 197

BONUS CHAPTER: WHEN YOU'RE LOOKING FOR STEAK, DON'T SETTLE FOR HAMBURGER 201

BIBLIOGRAPHY 207

CHAPTER ONE | WHAT DO YOU WANT TO DO WITH YOUR LIFE?

CHAPTER PURPOSE:
1. To START looking at career paths in a way that's different from the conventional advice you've been given.
2. To begin to connect what you love with what you want to achieve.

It's entirely normal, and accepted, for young people, especially in their early twenties – whether you've attended college or not, or currently attending – to be given strong advice from parents, loved ones, academic advisors, etc., to begin focusing on a career.

And while I think that's incredibly important, over the past few years, I'm beginning to think that advice is misguided. Yes, ultimately, we need to figure out what we should want to do in terms of our careers, but that's an outcome.

But maybe that's not the right way to START? Maybe there's a better way?

Now and again, you'll hear someone say: 'I missed my calling.' They say it in a joking way but they're really not joking.

Maybe there's a way for you to not miss your calling?

Granted, some of us know from an early age exactly what we want to do. And then we go and do it. But for most of us, it simply doesn't work that way. Or it doesn't quite work exactly the way we may think.

If you can take my advice here and begin to embrace this, I promise this will only help you better solidify possible career paths. This is not one of those things that has to feel like an alternative path to conventional thinking. Embracing this can't and won't hurt your thoughts.

I've thought about this for quite some time now, and I think if you begin to think about what you want to do with your life by asking yourself one question, you'll learn more about yourself and things can become clearer.

So, ask yourself what you want to do with your life…BUT…ask it within the following framework:

Do you want to:

- *Help people?*

- *Heal people?*

- *Fix something (that you think is broken with the world)?*

- *Make people laugh?*
- *Entertain people?*

- *Teach people?*

- *Influence people?*

- *Lead people?*

If you think the above is simplistic and vague; well, you're not completely wrong. But TRUST me.

Yes, it's vague but the bullet points you see here are meant to be PROMPTS. To get you to start thinking for yourself. So, it won't be vague once you begin to fill in the blanks.

The simplicity here is what I think adds to its effectiveness. Because I think too often, we are introduced serious ways for "serious" topics. And your career is serious. But if you start by **divorcing yourself from all the noise around you**, I think you'll be inspired. There's an innocence and a purity that I think comes with this exercise.

And its simplicity is also its strength when you think about it at a deep level.

And if these prompts aren't quite right for you, you can still use them as motivation for thinking about a different way to start.
Have you always liked and felt the need to 'tell' people things? Maybe you want to look at teaching?

Even though some of your friends may get tired of it, do you always seem to critique things, in a way that your critiques have important points, even when people disagree? Perhaps being a movie or food/restaurant critic is in your blood? No, seriously. Don't laugh.

Are you very good at taking material things and 'packaging' them in a way that adds new and further value? Maybe something in the real estate industry makes sense for you.

Again, let me remind you, all I'm saying is to use this as a START.

I'm sure you have a favorite actor, vocal artist, etc., and have seen interviews on them. Successful creative people seem to embrace this quite well. Almost all of them seem to talk about what they knew they wanted to do with their life, at a young age.

Al Pacino, in interviews, has talked about his given nick name at age 3, Sonny. And how family members used to watch him perform for them. Pacino has said that he knew he wanted to perform at a very early age.

George Carlin (my favorite comedian that I'll discuss in a separate chapter) used to say that he knew at an early age he wanted to entertain people. And at age 12 he begged his mother (who was a single mom that worked a lot to make ends meet) for his first microphone set. Since he badly wanted to be on the radio, the major medium when he was a kid.

Louis CK has talked about how he made the kids in class laugh in elementary school with just one joke when he was answering his teacher's question. And it was then that he knew what he wanted to do with his life: make people laugh.

And I realize that part of the outside noise has to do with how much money you can potentially make. To start, as well as a lifetime. Yes, that's super important. But that will begin to take shape as you go through this process first.

Besides, I'm old enough to have now seen many people chase a certain career because of the money. And while some seem content, I've seen so many people either leave a career or stay miserable – because they chased a career for the wrong reason(s).

If you're reading this book, you may not have a mortgage yet, or your own family, or a hundred other things you'll be responsible for later. Yes, life happens, and reality is <u>real</u>. **But you don't have to worry about those things yet!** So…This **IS** the time to try my best to help you embrace this.

THROW AWAY YOUR PLANS AND FOCUS INSTEAD ON GOALS

I love how ambitious, young people have plans.   A 5-year plan. A 10-year plan, etc.

Please rip them up and throw them in the garbage, literally. Or click delete on your computer and empty the little trash icon on the lower right of your screen. Now that we've got that out of the way…

Focus on goals instead. No, I promise this is not simply a difference in semantics.

And I will not dismiss plans – there IS value in them. And I said this wasn't just semantic differences – the way you look at plans vs. goals can very much shape your thinking – and the OUTCOME. Which is the whole point in the first place, right?

Ultimately, you're trying to accomplish things, yes?

In many aspects of your life (if not all), there is the end, and the means to an end.

The end is the goal. The means to that end is the plan.

The problem with many people is that they think they have the goal in mind, but they don't!

They have the plan much more figured out, because plans are much easier to formulate than goals. And that's why most people do that.

At the same time, plans are also susceptible to being flawed.

Part of the reason why plans are fundamentally flawed is because often they are planned years in advance. Life throws many curve balls at us, especially within the course of years.

The planning process, however, is much more valuable than any actual plan. Because the planning process (and a good one) includes contingencies and options as future things unfold.

Mike Tyson once famously said during an interview with a reporter:

"Everyone has a plan, until you get punched in the face."

Think about that for a minute. That's a lot of wisdom coming from a guy who wasn't necessarily known for being a strategic thinker (sorry, he's just not).

It shows the limited nature of plans and how plans and goals sometimes have a very distant relationship.

How about a similar quote from Dwight D. Eisenhower in 1957, when he was, by that time, President of the United States (after being Supreme Allied Commander of US Forces):

"Plans are worthless. But planning is everything."

Have you ever heard about the marshmallow challenge?

It's when groups of people are tasked with building a structure as tall as possible with a marshmallow on top without it collapsing.

There have been interesting studies over the years with this. Do you know what group consistently outperforms the MBA students?

Kindergarteners. The reason?

Although both the kindergartners and the MBA students have the same goal in mind, the kindergartners are a lot smarter when it comes to their plans.

The MBA students spend most of their time (it's a timed challenge) strategizing about the plan, because they naturally think it's all about focusing and agonizing on the plan. Only to find that once it comes to the goal – building their structures, they often fall a lot faster than intended.

The kindergarteners, on the other hand, only plan a bit. The spend most of their time on the goal. And they experiment and play with the time their allotted. They plan and then try. The marshmallow falls. And they learn from that and plan a little more, but then try to attain their goal again. They get more chances at their goal, and they wind up with taller structures than the MBA students.

If kindergartners taking MBA students to task with the marshmallow challenge isn't enough to convince you to plan, but not too much, well I'm not sure what will.

Goals are harder, partly because some people don't have the courage to commit or articulate their goals. Be confident enough to formulate and state your goals for others to know.

But where is the plan supposed to lead you? A lot of people have trouble with that.

Let's say you want to be wealthy (and there's nothing wrong with that). But remember, that's not a priority for everyone. Let's say it is for you. OK. So that's the goal. What's the plan?
The plan, the route, the strategy to become wealthy is not a linear path! There are so many ways to become wealthy. Hell, there are even many illegal ways! But no, do it the legal way. But there are many legal ways to achieve that goal.

You need to start with goals.

Plans are, by their very nature, linear and even "technical." But by creating a plan, you've created some type of linear path from where you are now to where you want to go. Life doesn't work like that.

Another issue with plans is that they're often too 'traditional.'

There is simply far too much dogma built into many plans.

And sometimes taking an unorthodox approach to things allows you to be the game changer, the trail blazer, the revolutionary.

Goals are spatial and strategic. They are so much better and powerful. Goals aren't linear. A goal considers that there might be several paths to ultimately get to the same destination. And goals also consider that sometimes the goals themselves – **change.**

There is only one constant in life. Change.
Life is fluid. Notice I didn't say "life is full of ups and downs." Well, it is, but you don't need to hear that from me. And the idiot that invented that saying probably didn't know much about life if that's the best they could come up with.

When you look at your life in terms of a plan, you're setting yourself up for potential failure and disappointment.

HAPPY ACCIDENTS

I came up with a term about ten years ago that just seemed to be natural: Happy accidents. They are unintended, positive outcomes that can come out of focusing on goals as opposed to plans.

They can come at any time and in any size – meaning they can be small, little things on the side or perhaps start that way and wind up being big things that may change the trajectory of your life. Or anything in between.

When you have your goals in mind but are flexible with your plans, interesting twists and turns come your way, literally. They flow around in the air around you and come at you when you least expect them.

Happy accidents are so freaking awesome. I've experienced this a few times throughout life.

DON'T DAYDREAM

If you're over the age of around 12 or so, the first thing I would ask you to do is stop daydreaming. Let's face it – we ALL daydream when we're young. Whether you're a guy or young lady, daydreaming is almost built in.

Daydreaming, while you're lying on your bed in the middle of a Saturday or Sunday afternoon feels pretty good, saying to yourself that you're going to do *this* and achieve *that* – but there's one problem. It doesn't do anything. Daydreaming costs nothing since when you're young you have your entire life ahead of you. But it also doesn't offer any pay off.

You know how you get things done? By doing them. By literally moving your arms and legs and starting the first step.

You don't owe it to your parents, friends, a promise to a dying grandparent, someone special, your Aunt Sally, etc.

You owe it to **yourself**.

Let me also say upfront...I'm sorry to tell you because this seems to bother some people. But HOPE is not a plan. It's just not.

Don't get me wrong, there is a lot of use in hope. And there are some very useful motivational talks out there on YouTube, TED, etc. (and many lousy ones, too), but the ones that are good can only go as far as doing one thing: motivating you.

You can use hope, as part of prayer (and I am happy to say I pray a few times a week, and have been for years), but hope should come after your plan. When your life isn't going in the direction you want it to (and believe me, I've been there – more than once), you need to examine your behaviors and see what things you need to change. In other words, you need to take a personal inventory.

See, aren't you happy that I didn't simply tell you some stupid, worthless crap such as 'put your big girl/big boy pants on and deal with it?' That's hot shot, nonsense talk. I hate hot shots.

I think most of us know when we are going through a period of our lives where, quite frankly, we are just not doing our best. We are not taking full ownership on the things we can control.

Check out the chapter on ownership, where I'll elaborate in a slightly different way. But you can tie it all in.

CHAPTER TWO | SELF-AWARENESS

CHAPTER PURPOSE:
- Self-awareness is the single most important trait to develop when you're young.

The most important thing that you can learn when you are young boils down to one thing: self-awareness. I promise you, promise you, promise you. (Did I promise you)?

Self-awareness has to do with your ability to not only understand your surroundings, but how you fit in those surroundings. It also has a lot to do with how people perceive you. If you can understand these two things within a context, you're halfway there. **And I sincerely think you're going places in life.**

Before I continue, let me just say that this comes a bit more naturally for certain people than others. But it's something that we can ALL learn and continue to get better at. It's a learnable skill.

While self-awareness is super important in your personal and professional life, one of the biggest skills that employers are looking for from young graduates as well as young people with a few years of experience is very much your self-awareness. Employers realize you may not have any hard experience in the industry yet, but they're looking for how aware of yourself and your surroundings you are. Because the more aware you are, the more successful you'll probably be.

As juvenile as this may sound, remember the 'cool kids' in high school? Yes, they may be the cool kids because they are the best looking (guys and girls), they are athletes, etc., but the cool kids do have one additional thing going for them that's underrated: self-awareness. Even if they're completely superficial (and that's not always the case, by the way), they're aware of how they achieved their social status and how to hold on to. In its own way, it's better than being an awkward high school student that's not only unsure of themselves but how they fit in.

Some people are born with a better sense of this (we all have certain talents given to us at birth) and some people learn self-awareness faster, such as student athletes. The reason why athletes tend to understand this a bit faster is due to the competitive nature of athletics and the necessity to take a "hard" inventory of themselves.

So, let's talk about what a hard inventory entails. A hard inventory means assessing all your strong points and your weaknesses. NOW, I realize that using the word "weaknesses" is no longer PC (politically correct) and it's been replaced with the word "opportunities." But I'm trying to truly help you here, so let's get a little "raw" and keep it as is. Many of us have a good grasp on our strong points, so that's the easy one. We need to focus on our weaknesses. We have a vague, general idea of our weaknesses. And sometimes when our weaknesses are the reason why we didn't get a job, for example, they become temporarily emphasized. But then we go back to placing them on the back shelf and they become a bit vague again.

So how do you become self-aware or further self-aware? I think the answer is a dynamic made of several things, all intertwined.

Feedback and being a good listener:

I'll add these two together since there's no need to separate them. The most important piece is being open to receiving constructive feedback and taking the action points that come out of that feedback to focus on. If you're (hopefully) receiving constructive feedback, whether it's formal, such as a job. Or informal, such as friends, it should be a mix of positive and things you can improve on. The positive ones are easy, but remember, they're positive; so, you don't need to focus and work on those.

Focus on the areas of improvement and look for patterns. If various people (different bosses, different groups of friends, etc.) are sort of saying the same thing, then there's probably something to it. Forgive me if this is too on the surface, but I consistently see this happen so it's worth mentioning. Do your best to not be overly defensive when receiving feedback. I think it's OK to DEFEND yourself, to an extent. Just don't be overly defensive.

I once worked at a smaller-sized company where there were about 60 employees at the time. I managed a team of five individuals: a combination of product development associates and technical designers. The head technical designer was a talented person, and she had not only solid experience but knew how to generally get things done.

It was time to provide annual feedback, and the overwhelming number of constructive feedback/areas for improvement were her interpersonal skills. She wanted to be a one-person show, an island, essentially.

She was good at her job but didn't work well with her co-workers and didn't align with me on some of the "bigger," major initiatives before going into various rabbit holes, etc. During her annual feedback session, she was unfortunately far too defensive on almost every issue I had on paper. There was one issue where her defensiveness came in handy, and I did learn something new from her perspective and she had a great point. I acknowledged that immediately. But it was a difficult performance appraisal to deliver, because on every other issue she over-defended herself when it wasn't necessary. What wound up happening is that I had to give her feedback not only on her annual performance but feedback on how she was handling the review, too.

When receiving feedback and taking a hard inventory, it's thinking time, not feeling time. (Sorry if that was corny).

PERCEPTION

I know the concept has been covered quite extensively, but the next issue is perception. And yes, as the saying goes, PERCEPTION IS REALITY. It's more than just a saying, unfortunately. I truly wish this wasn't true, but it is. And I live in the same world as you, so I can only share the rules with you.

I'm mainly referring to how people perceive you, more than how you perceive them. This is about your self-awareness, not analyzing others.

Some people love that perception is reality. The reason is simple:

They are life-long bullshitters.

When you're full of shit, then perception being reality can go in your favor for a long time. But hopefully you're not that, so you'll need a plan.

Going back to feedback for just a second, if people give you input on how you're being perceived by others, well that's a good start. This isn't always the case, but sometimes it does happen. When it comes to people giving you feedback on how you're perceived, as opposed to other types of general feedback, on this I don't think there's any room for defensiveness. Because whatever you think, in this context, doesn't matter (unfortunately). At the time when hearing how you're perceived, unfortunately it doesn't matter if it's based on the truth, a misunderstanding, a lie, or even a ridiculous, blatant lie. You can address those things as needed. But you need to accept what others think of you.

Can I throw in some quick humor for a second? I know Louis C.K. got himself in trouble with the MeToo Movement but he did an act about 10 years ago that was funny and addressed this issue directly.

He said, "You know when people say you're an asshole and you respond with 'NO, I'M NOT.' Well, it's not up to you!"

Hopefully that helps solidify the point.

BRUTAL HONESTY WITH YOURSELF

The first thing I'd say is that you'll need to be brutally honest with yourself. And here's the good news about this; you don't necessarily need to be honest with others as you go through this process. Some people may already know what's holding you back, and some don't. But they don't matter. You do. If it makes you feel better (and I hope it does), being honest with yourself is an internal process. You don't have to reveal things to others.

But you will need to be honest. We all BS ourselves, to some extent. <u>But you can't BS yourself on this</u>. If you try and BS yourself with this, don't even bother. Because it won't work.

TAKING PERSONAL INVENTORY

Hopefully you'll be brutally honest with yourself, and next you'll need to take a good inventory and ask yourself what is it you want? That will begin to give you a pathway as to how to get it.

Notice, I'm not describing this as one of those 12-step processes, and I'm purposely not using terms such as "step 1," "step 2," etc. Granted, there is a chronology to the process, but this is fluid, not linear.

STOP THE EXCUSES AND DETERMINE ROOT CAUSE

You'll need to understand what the root cause of what you don't like first is.

If you don't like your job, I'm not going to suggest that you necessarily go out and find a new one – at least NOT yet. Because the reason why you don't like your job might not be about your job. It might be about you.

If you're not getting good grades, in general, is it really because of your professors, or the school? Or is it more about you?

If you're in a bad relationship, is it because the other person is at fault and they have a thousand issues and you have none, because it's not you? Well, maybe you want to think twice before concluding it's the other person. Again, it might be the other person, but not so fast.

Determining what the real problem is that lies underneath is critical to changing the direction of your life. So how to you put together a roadmap to do that?

I'm going to do my best here and utilize some of the skills I learned as a sociology student when I was an undergrad to help you.

I think cause and effect will help you understand what's going on and how to change things.

Most of our poor choices and (sometimes) poor behaviors and lifestyle choices are effects, not causes. And I must stress again, when it comes to changing the trajectory of your life, most things really do boil down to...you. Remember, as I started this chapter: There's only one way to change your life, change your behaviors.

Don't worry, the world doesn't have it "in for you."

If you begin to change your behaviors, things will directionally start to go in your favor. They really will.

Do you find that most of the time when you meet someone and begin a relationship, it winds up going downhill in a short amount of time? It's not because you're unlucky.

Do you find that in general, you never seem to be in a financially positive situation, and even during times you come into some extra money you still seem to wind up financially 'even,' or where you started, at best?

Do you find that in every job you've had, the same issues pop up? Hmm...I think that's a pattern, don't you?

Stop blaming others. Stop blaming your "horrible" boss, co-workers, professors, etc.

Take ownership. You really need to OWN this. As I said, you owe it to yourself.

I think you need to start investing in yourself. You've heard this before. But when you invest in yourself in better choices (cause) you'll get better outcomes (effect).

Think of it like this: Aren't you tired of spending time talking about what you want instead of working on doing it? Can I tell you something? Ask people who are older than you – what their number 1 issue is with not trying to make changes in their life. I'll bet money that they will all say one thing: **Regret**.

Getting out of your comfort zone means that you are willing to cope/not afraid, in the short term, with the following:

- Pain of rejection

- Pain of failure
- Pain of disappointment

Yes, these WILL be painful in the short term. They just will. But I can tell you something that I've learned from actors (I've never done any acting, but I know a little about the business).

Now granted, maybe actors aren't necessarily trying to change the direction of their lives and they're simply trying to make it in show business, but I think this still works, to share with you. Actors are completely fine with rejection, failure, and disappointment. They must be. Do you know how many times the big-name actors fail before they get their "big break?"

CHAPTER THREE | DEAR BIG MOUTHS (LIKE ME), THIS ONE'S FOR YOU

CHAPTER PURPOSE:
1. How becoming a good listener can truly change your life.
2. How to learn STRATEGIC communication skills.

I was originally going to name this chapter "Listen More, Talk Less." But I felt that wouldn't truly capture some of the points I want to discuss.

There are several parts here. First, learning how to develop and modulate to what extent you communicate and discuss topics. And the second part, equally important, is learning the ability to listen. I also included additional communication issues that are worthy of discussion.

So, let's start with some basics. And this is for you, not me, but pretty much my entire life, people have told me that I have a big mouth. And they're right. But don't you hate when people (no matter what the subject), even friends and family, state one of your flaws but that's all they do? They don't help you, right?

Well, if you have a big mouth, like me, I have some practical advice that you can apply that will help you.

In the same way it's helped me over the past five or six years.

Talking too much really can be a hindrance to you. When I was in my twenties, I didn't realize that or fully understand that. But it can be a negative in not only your personal relationships, but also work ones. And it can have negative consequences. You probably won't lose friends (because they are, after all your friends) but I can bet that talking too much and being perceived as a big mouth can cause you to not have as many friends as you could. And it can also be the one differentiating reason as to why you didn't get the job, or the promotion.

People who talk too much will probably always talk more than others, and in some ways (some) that may be OK. We shouldn't desire to change ourselves completely. But we can improve once we realize one key issue that finally dawned on me.

For those who talk too much are usually very interested and intense on certain issues and topics in life (the older I get the more I hate the word "passion" and that's why I'm not using it). What we need to understand and accept, even though it's sometimes a hard pill to swallow at first, is that not everyone is going to care about the topics we talk about as much as we do. It takes some practice, but it will become more natural to you as time goes on.

In my presentations book, *It's Called Presenting, Not Talking Out Loud*, I talk a lot about understanding your audience. And this is the same thing, in principle. Your audience can be one hundred people or your parents and aunts and uncles at the Thanksgiving table, or just one person you're having a casual conversation with.

For example, even if we're talking to someone who's interested in the topic at hand as we are, we need to accept that they may not be AS INTERESTED as we are. They want to hear about, and discuss the topic, too. But only to a certain extent. Of course, sometimes you'll have a person who's just as interested in a topic as much as you. And when that happens, great! But most of the time we need to develop our ability to gauge how much they want to discuss something, and at a certain point, we need to learn how to STOP!

It's going to take practice, and of course, there's no conceivable way I could tell you when that stopping point will be. I'm not with you, nor do I know the topic or your audience. But what I can PROMISE you is with practice, if you become self-conscious of this, you WILL get better.

And the results are SO WORTH IT.

Another way to improve your skills of talking less has to do with a different element of understanding your audience. I'll never forget this mistake I made when I was around 24 or so. I started a small side business where I took my experience in print advertising sales and decided to start my own monthly restaurant guide. I did progress to the point where I published two issues, but I then moved on to other things (this was the early to mid 2000s and there was no such term as "side hustle" or "side gig" back then).

Anyway, one of my friend's fathers has been an entrepreneur and small business owner almost his whole life. And one night I was dropping my friend off and was invited to stay for dinner. My friend's parents and his grandparents were also over. My friend's dad said he heard about the magazine and asked me about it at the dinner table. He sincerely asked, and I was so eager to share, but I shared too many details for too long.

After a while my friend's dad politely said something to the effect that other people at the table want to have a conversation about other things. Once he said that, I understood. And to this day I feel a bit embarrassed when I think about it. It was his polite way of telling me to shut up and that he and everyone else heard enough. I was too young to understand that at the time. It's part of the learning process, especially when you're in your twenties.

But by reading this at least you get a head start, since no one had told me!

BECOME A GOOD LISTENER, AND SEE THE BENEFITS POUR IN

The second part of this chapter has to do with another interconnected issue – maybe think of this as the flip side of talking less. And it's all about listening more.

As I said in my presentation skills book, people LOVE to talk about themselves. Humans are wired that way. And one way in which you can become a trusted, well-respected person and someone that others RELY ON is to become a better listener.

I have to say; it works wonders.

When you begin to become a good listener, and I know this sounds a little corny, it almost becomes MAGICAL. You almost can't believe how powerful this skill is!

I'm also going to be brutally honest here and I think I know what some of you might be thinking. And no, I must firmly state that this is NOT about manipulating people and taking advantage of them. Do manipulators also have this one skill of coming across as good listeners? Maybe. But their agenda is much different. Their mirage of being a good listener is all about pretending to care. Their version of being a good listener is analogous to the child molester who offers a child candy and is kind to them for the first five minutes before they convince them to get inside their car.

A genuinely good listener may need to give more "airtime" to the speaker, especially when they have much they want to say. But if you begin to develop a reputation with people (which implies some type of longer-term relationship, different than the manipulator) you'll also notice:

By being a good listener, people will give you MORE of their attention when it's time for them to listen to you. And they'll respect you a lot more. Again, they trust you. People love to talk about themselves. And you provided them that. And now they'll listen to you, with less effort and more attention than they would, otherwise.

Invest in becoming a good listener, and this skill will pay off your entire life, again and again.

DON'T TELL PEOPLE THINGS THEY ALREADY KNOW

Since we're talking about STRATEGIC COMMUNICATION in this chapter, I thought this would be a good place to also talk about something that many young people do. And once again, I know it's unintentional.

Back to knowing your audience, no matter how big or small they are, an important skill to learn as early as you can in life is to understand what someone already REASONABLY knows.

Notice I said REASONABLY. I'm not suggesting that each person you speak to needs to be googled and researched in advance, like some damn job interview; I get that. So don't worry about that. I'm not necessarily talking about facts and figures. What I mean is to be as self-aware as you possibly can be and make a reasonable, natural assessment of what people already know, or may know.

And then make sure you don't tell them those things. Assume they know.

When you tell people things they already know, I can't really think of a scenario where any good can come out of that. When you do that, people will probably think you are:

- Arrogant
- Wasting their time
- And just an all-around know-it-all

And that's if they LIKE you. Yes, like you. If they don't like you, they'll think of you as:

- Smug
- Cocky
- A smart-ass little shit

Nobody likes a know-it-all. Not even you, right? So, there you go!

If you're an ambitious young business student and chatting with someone who owns a bar about your ideas to "revolutionize" the bar business, go for it! You may be on to something, and I mean that. Just focus on your wonderful ideas immediately, right out of the gate. **Don't tell a bar owner who's been in the business for 30 years about how the bar business works.** You'll lose their attention before you even start.

If you're having a business conversation with your boss or perhaps your bosses' boss about all your wonderful ideas, since you're a young whippersnapper (I've never known what the hell that means, by the way), don't provide basic things about the business or industry. They already know. If you need to provide some background for context, OK, that makes sense. But don't provide them with unnecessary information and waste their time.

If you're having a discussion with your friends, they're your peers, right? And you typically can assume what they know so you don't need to tell them things they already know...just tell them the "new" stuff. So, it's really the same thing with all audiences – do your best to assess what you think they most likely already know.

When you have conversations with people and assume they already know certain things about the general subject, they will be so much MORE interested in listening to you and your POINT. I promise this will happen. No question about it.

Sometimes, there's nothing wrong with asking someone if they're familiar with a particular aspect of a topic, that's fine. That can also be viewed as a positive, since by way of you asking, you're showing them that you don't want to waste their time. Use your best judgment on that one.

One of the tactics I use in my professional life, when I'm unsure if someone knows some background info, I'll start with "In case you didn't know..." and then quickly explain something. When you say "in case" you're not making people feel ignorant. It's a neutral way to start. I've been given feedback that phrasing things that way was appreciated.

OFFENSE VS. DEFENSE

There are two ways you can look at this section. Offense vs. defense. Or proactive vs. reactive.

The pair of words you use really depends on the context. If you're thinking that the proactive/reactive pair is a bit more positive and the offense/defense pair seems a bit more "combative," I'd probably agree with that.

It's best that you're proactive, for the most part.

Always try to DO. Do, do, do. Do new things in your job, do innovate things. Try new things. Meet new friends, etc., etc. That's all proactive.

One thing I've learned about life is the more you do, in whatever aspect that means, the better. You're just doing – doing your thing. You're making the decisions. While this may seem a little corny, you're controlling your own destiny. No really, you are. That wasn't meant to be philosophical. I mean it in a very down-to-earth way.

Here's the most important thing to understand about being defensive:

When you need to be defensive, and sometimes we all must, **you aren't in as much control as you wish.**

Someone or something has put you in a defensive situation. Because when you're placed in a position of defense, or forced to react, you need to answer things, issues, etc. It's an awful feeling.

Even if you can defend yourself to the fullest, it's still not a desired position to be in.

A lot of this boils down to how much control over things you have in your life. It doesn't have to mean you're a "controlling" person. I mean, if you are, OK. But we all want to be in control of as many things in our life as we possibly can.

FACTS VS. EMOTIONS

Let me start off with an important confession. I'm an emotional person. Everyone that knows me, knows this. I've become a little better over the years, but my general disposition of being an emotional person probably won't ever change.

And over the years, emotion has gotten me into a lot of trouble (a lot). I don't mean trouble with the law or anything like that, I just mean trouble.

I promised this book is about you, not me. But I needed to tell you that upfront. If I didn't, I wouldn't be able to write this section – and would feel like a hypocrite.

The division president (now COO of the overall corporation) of a company I used to work at, who I got to know a little and traveled with to China, would always tell us to stick to the facts when dealing with issues.

Granted, I don't know him personally, but I can tell he is not as emotional as I am. This comes easier for him – and some of you. For some of us, we must work at it.

His advice, however, was invaluable. Every time I stuck to the facts; the outcome of the situation turned out better than it would have otherwise. Every time.

As I continued to embrace this, I was able to eventually articulate my thoughts:

It's not personal unless it's personal.

And when it comes to business issues, 99% of the time, it's not personal.

When you get emotional about issues that don't call for it, here's what generally happens:

- There's a genuine disconnect between you and the other person (or issue) at hand. In other words, people don't know why you're acting the way you are. You're not focused.

- You're not effectively communicating your side of the story since the emotion is getting the best of you – and people are hearing "noise" on their end. And I'm sure you do have a valid issue, but you're not able to get the message through.
- Sometimes people do know why you're acting the way you are, but they TRULY don't care. Not a lick!

- You may open yourself up to far too much interpretation. This will most likely be an issue for your reputation in the future and may also shed light on some of the things you did in the past (in a negative way) and some people will begin to connect certain dots.

- You can genuinely anger the other person. I don't just mean frustrating them or hurting your credibility in the process. With some issues, you may genuinely anger them, as well.

One of the benefits that I've noticed with sticking to the facts is that you can take down the overall emotion by a few notches, immediately.

You can take a situation that's currently at a '9' or '10' and bring it down to at least a '6.'

At a '9,' you can't have any dispute resolution and there's steam coming out of your ears. At a '6,' you can hopefully have a PRODUCTIVE conversation.

When you stick to the facts, as a baseline, you are far more focused and SPECIFIC. Sorry if this is overly simplistic but think about someone threatening to take you to court and sue you for breach of contract (civil litigation). Which one of these statements would concern you more?

I'm going to take you to court and sue you for every penny you have, every penny you'll ever make, and every penny your children and grandchildren will ever make! Your grandchildren will spit on your grave for what you'll have done to them!

Or

I'm going to take you to court and sue you for breach of contract. You owe me a balance of 50% of promised royalties for the last two years. You only started paying me full royalties, per our agreement, *starting this year. We also agreed in the contract that if sales doubled between year 1 and year 2 (which they did), I'd be entitled to an additional $50,000 lump sum payment – payable 30 days after the close of year 2. We're now in the second half of year 3!*

Which one of these statements do you think you'd get more nervous about? Hopefully the latter.

The former is tougher but just emotion – it's SMACK TALK.

The latter is sobering, specific, and serious.

I know this may sound weird (and I really hope this isn't taken completely out of context) but now and again I'll catch one of those documentaries on illicit drugs/drug dealers. I'm sure many of you have also seen some. They're interesting on a boring Saturday or Sunday afternoon.

I hate to say this, but I have respect (relatively speaking) for some of the drug dealers who are wearing a bandana to hide their face while telling their side. The film maker will ask them about evading the police, etc., and the drug dealer will be very calm and essentially say something to the effect of: the police have a job to do (which is catch us), and we have a job to do (sell drugs). Sometimes the police win and sometimes the drug dealers win. And that's how they see it.

There's something about looking at it like that, that makes me feel those are the "smarter" drug dealers.

They're not being emotional about it. They're being rational. They're doing their job.

DON'T EXAGGERATE

In some practical ways, I think you can look at exaggeration as a mix between facts and emotion. I know that we often exaggerate to help advance our perspective. But in most cases, exaggeration doesn't help.

I think that when we exaggerate positive things, that's somewhat harmless. Or if not harmless, it's far less harmful than when we exaggerate negative things.

When you exaggerate:

- You lose general credibility.
- People often know you're exaggerating.

You also overshoot your issue. And sometimes that can mean you will get less than what you wanted. And I hate to say this but sometimes that means you may get nothing. In other words, things can completely **backfire** on you. They really can.

And if either of these things happen, you'll surely be embarrassed. The more people and the more you expose yourself, if things don't go your way, the more you'll embarrass yourself.

When you don't exaggerate, you can at least be reasonably assured that you won't be at all embarrassed. And you'll almost definitely get more, keep as much credibility, and as much respect and dignity for yourself as you can.

DON'T TEAR PEOPLE APART

Most of the time, even when someone has done you wrong, or when someone asks you your opinion on someone who did you wrong, you had a bad experience, etc., my advice is to not tear the person apart.

Please excuse my language but you know the phrase, 'rip them a new asshole?' Don't do that. It's not necessary. Plus, wouldn't that hurt the person like a mother f'er?

When you do that, **you're saying more about yourself rather than them**. And everything and anything credible that lives somewhere within the middle of your emotional rant, will get lost.

When you're, for the most part rationale when complaining about someone, you not only show that you're being analytical, but you're being productive with your words. It shows you're a leader – or future leader. Because you have the ability to not just look at one thing without the greater context.

You can have a 'tone,' sure. Stay human. You're not a robot. But either keep it a tone, or if you're going to share a bit of emotion, share just a bit, and probably at the end.

You're also showing that your analytical when you're balanced. I've had dinner conversations with SVPs, CEOs, etc. And some of the smartest people I've ever spoken to – even when they "hate" someone, will offer some degree of balance, and bring up their good points, too.

There's a guy I know who was the SVP of Product Development and Sourcing at one of the companies I've worked at, and then became EVP at another company. I was having dinner with him about eight years ago and we were talking about the VP of

Product Development and Sourcing at the company I was working at, at the time.

He had hired the VP personally since he knew him for twenty years. Their relationship somehow soured over the years (it's complicated, but typical, in corporate).

Although their relationship had gone south, and the SVP was personally upset, since they had a genuine twenty-year friendship, he still managed to bring up the VP's good points.

I've always remembered that throughout the years. It was a memorable and teaching moment for me. The ability to separate emotions from objective qualities of an individual – even when both men also had a personal, long-term friendship. It showed genuine maturity and intelligence.

SPEAKING IN THE AFFIRMATIVE

I wouldn't have written a section on this if I didn't find the issue pervasive. Too many young people will literally begin to answer a question or discuss something by talking about the negation of a certain topic.

You'll generally always be more effective when you speak in the affirmative, not the negative. I find this to be a very common issue that won't serve you well if you don't practice changing this habit.

For the most part, speak FOR things, not against them. Don't tell people what you don't like. Tell people what you LIKE!

Let me start with this example and I promise I'll make it more sophisticated, and we'll kick it up a few notches.

If I ask you where you prefer to go in the summer, the beach, or the lake, and if you like the beach and don't really like the lake, that's fine. **Don't talk about why you don't like going to the lake.** Spend the time talking about why you like going to the beach!

You'll be surprised at how many people spend time talking about why they don't like the lake.

Sometimes it's easier to talk about things we don't like. And harder to talk about things we like. I think part of that has to do with confidence – but you can change that if you just change your mentality. And after some time, you'll notice a change in you.

If you like the beach instead of the lake, look at the difference between these two statements:

Affirmative:
I really enjoy going to the beach during the summer. I love watching the waves and to breathe in that salt air. I like finding a nice spot...with my chair, my cooler, my music, and a magazine. The sand, the surf, the beach bar, and that "fun" atmosphere...that's for me!

Negative:
I don't like the lake. I don't like to fish, or hike, or anything like that. Whether it's a tent or cabin, the "rustic" scene doesn't work for me. I know the lake can be fun, but even when it's nice and warm in the summer, I have to pack a jacket because it will get cold in the evening. Wearing flip flops and shorts during the day and needing to wear pants and a jacket at night.

Do you see the difference? It's night and day. These are worlds apart. There are so many reasons why you should generally speak in the affirmative:

- Your language and words are simply more effective and engaging.

- You'll show that you stand for something.

- By not being on the defensive about an issue, it will emphatically prove to whomever is listening to you that you truly care and are committed to whatever it is you're talking about.

Think deeply about this last bullet point for a moment, please. If you find yourself having more to say about why you don't like the lake, and not nearly as many positive things about why you the beach, people won't have much faith and conviction in you. **Think about why they asked you that question in the first place.** And they won't take you as seriously as you want them to.

I think, and hope, you see the big difference.

OK, now let's kick it up a notch...

I know many people don't like politics but please indulge me for a moment.

There was a politician in a recent general election that was running against a man with a unique personality, and she never really seemed to tell you **why** you should vote for her. She spent the bulk of her time trying to tell you why you shouldn't vote for him.

Does this make much sense to you? It doesn't to me. Don't get me wrong! There's a place to talk about why you shouldn't vote for him (I'll explain more of that below) but in general – a politician should talk about why you should vote for them.

What if a family member or close friend was in the market to buy a new car, and they asked you for your advice since they respect your opinion. They're thinking about Car A or Car B. In your mind, you'd like them to buy Car A. What do you think is more effective? Talking about all the negatives of Car B? Or all the positives of Car A?

OK, now let's get to the middle – that "in between" speaking in the affirmative vs. defensively, where it depends on the context:

If you emigrated to the United States from a different country and someone asks you why you moved to the US, what makes more sense? To discuss why you left your native country or why you moved to the United States?

If someone is asking you in a positive manner as to why you moved to the US, my strong suggestion is to explain all the things you like about the US. Because that's what will resonate with them. If you talk about all the reasons why you left your former country, that's important, **but did you really answer their question?**

Think about that for a moment. You probably didn't answer their question if you answered in that manner.

And think about it this way. If you shared the negative aspects of your country and why you left, they may empathize but can't really relate, since they most likely have never been to your country. They'll empathize (or try to) but it won't be genuine. They're just listening to you talk at that point, they aren't relating to your words.

However, if someone who is from **your native country** asks why you moved to the US, you're most likely to provide them with reasons as to why you left. Because that's what most likely resonates with them. And I'd bet money that's probably the motivation for their question.

THE EXCEPTION – WHEN TO FOCUS ON THE NEGATIVE AND BE DEFENSIVE

OK, I just explained how you should speak in the affirmative most of the time. But, in fairness, I also owe you the flip side.

Of course, there are times when you need to discuss why you don't like something.

A lot of times will boil down to the **intent** of the person asking the question. As you gain more life experience, you'll be able to better gauge the **motivation** of someone asking you a question in the first place.

When it comes to topics that you can speak in both the affirmative and the negative, speak in the negative when you need to defend yourself against people ATTACKING you.

If someone asks or criticizes your decision for moving into the suburbs as opposed to the nearest major city (such as New York, San Francisco, Boston, etc.), **they don't give a damn about the reasons why you moved to the suburbs. <u>That's when you need to become defensive.</u>**

Don't take the "moral high ground" and be nice by stating in the affirmative why you chose the suburbs. That won't resonate with the person attacking you.

You need to defend your decision. You need to shut that person down – and tell them maybe 20% of why you moved to the suburbs, but 80% why you didn't move into the city. That's, after all, why they asked you the question in the first place.

I promised you the straight dope in this book. And I don't want to come across as mean. But sometimes...

You just need to shut some people down.

A lot of people think that you should always take the moral high ground and be professional. Not always.

Another issue that young people tend to have, which is directly related, is to begin to explain something that was asked of them by explaining its opposite.

Let me ask you: If someone who's never tasted it before asks you about chocolate ice cream, are you going to explain it by talking about vanilla? What the hell, right? Does that help answer their question?

No offense, please, don't do that.

I think there are a few reasons this happens:

1. Sometimes it's easier to start that way (and I can respect that).

2. Sometimes you don't have a good, confident grasp of the question, so you try to compensate with a somewhat related, but different answer on something that wasn't asked for.

3. You simply haven't been trained better, and not enough people have helped correct that.

    For example, I've asked marketing questions such as the following in class. For those of you who are not in marketing or who've never taken a marketing class, don't worry – it doesn't take away from the point:

    Can someone tell us what horizontal conflict is?

    And I've received this type of answer far too many times (no joke):

    Well, first, <u>vertical</u> conflict is when companies are in separate channels and were originally designed to be complementary, are now competing with one another, such as a price issue, etc.

*AND THEN, HOPEFULLY, THEY'LL BEGIN TO TALK ABOUT **HORIZONTAL** CONFLICT (HOPEFULLY).*

With all due respect, that's NOT what I asked!

I asked about <u>horizontal</u> conflict. Not vertical. If I wanted to ask you about vertical conflict, I would have. When you do the above, you really need to understand that by not answering what was asked, you are wasting the listener's time.

Sorry to be blunt, but yes, wasting. And since you spent a few sentences explaining vertical conflict, I won't say, but there's a decent chance that your answer for horizontal conflict won't be all that good, to be honest.

CHAPTER FOUR | OWNERSHIP IS THE WAY TO A FULFILLING LIFE

CHAPTER PURPOSE:
1. Feeling a genuine sense of ownership allows you to gain more confidence.
2. Ownership allows you to better connect with the world, and more likely to be in control of more things in your life.
3. Ownership is much stronger than happiness. Happiness is a byproduct. Ownership is an input.
4. Don't be afraid to LOVE things.

I'll start this chapter by sharing something sincere. I've thought a lot (and will continue to think) about what makes a life worth living. And let me be clear. As much as I loved studying Socrates and Plato as an undergrad, I do NOT mean this in a philosophical way, but in a very pragmatic one. And I've finally come to a simple conclusion:

I want to matter.

And I hope you do, too.

I want to matter to people. I want things to matter. And I want to matter to things. Not just anything, but some thing(s).

This chapter is NOT about ownership of material things, such as owning a home or an apartment.

Those things are good if you want them. But I'm not that superficial and irresponsible to write something like that in a book. Nor am I trying to be Suze Orman and provide you with personal finance advice (which, by the way, only half is of any value).

What I mean by ownership being the path to the most fulfilling life is to OWN ideas, concepts, practices, etc. You have **every right to own things**, and others don't get the right to have a patent on them. Unless they have an actual patent for a product or service, then be careful. I don't want you to get sued ☺.

Let me first get this out of the way, because you might be thinking that happiness is the goal to life.

Happiness is so overrated, it's ridiculous.

Happiness is NOT a goal. It's just not. Happiness is an outcome or at best, a byproduct. A byproduct can't be a goal. That doesn't make sense. I'm not suggesting that you shouldn't desire to be happy; you should if you want. But I need to reiterate that **happiness is not a goal**.

The things you do, whatever they may be, hopefully can make you happy. You can't start the day by saying you want to be happy. You can, however, start the day by saying you want to achieve x, y, or z, and achieving those things will hopefully also offer you happiness.

Sometimes young people tend to say that they're PASSIONATE about something. And while I've written in a separate section of this book why passion is overrated, it's a good place to start.

When you're passionate about something, whether it lasts your entire life or temporary, these are things you not only care about, but more importantly – things that you LOVE.

And things that you LOVE should be things that you OWN. I'm not that much of a spiritual person, but I can tell you I've learned that fulfillment in life comes from things that matter to you the most. Not just conceptually, but in practice, of some kind. You want to be able to own a space in the world. And I'm dead serious.

To me, fulfillment is stronger than happiness. While happiness can be real, it can also be fake (when we fool ourselves that we're happy). And happiness can also be temporary. Fulfillment isn't something you can trick yourself with. It's permanent and rewarding.

When you own something, or certain things, and become some sort of authority, the fulfillment and how it makes you feel is incredible. It's better than sex. And lasts a hell of a lot longer.

You don't have to be an official authority. If you wind up being one, great, but you don't have to. You just need to be an authority, in some way.

Do you know pretty much everything there is to know about make up, beauty, and personal care? And yes, even as a guy, I realize there are millions of women on YouTube with their own beauty channels. Too many, to be honest. But so what?! Are you known to be a beauty maven?

Forget about the Kardashians – they're half full of shit, anyway. You don't have to be them. If you're a beauty expert, whether you can make it official or not, be a beauty expert. OWN that space. Don't take a passive approach to your beauty knowledge. Even if you don't turn it into a business or a huge YouTube channel (which would be great, if you can) own that space. It doesn't just **belong** to certain people. It's **YOURS TOO**!

Do you love working on cars, and for example, maybe understand everything there is to know about working on and repairing a certain car brand? OWN that space.

Not far from where I grew up, in northern New Jersey, there's an auto repair shop which I won't name. Not because of possible libel issues but because I don't give ANYONE free advertising ☺.

But they're in Bergen County, NJ and specialize in the repair of Mercedes-Benz, any year. That's the only brand they work on, which can be risky to alienate so many other customers. But that's what they've decided to do. The owner is a certified Mercedes-Benz master technician, who loves and knows everything about these cars. He used to work in a Mercedes-Benz dealership and then decided to quit and open his own shop. Mercedes-Benz (the company) is NOT the only one who gets to love and understand Mercedes-Benz.

DON'T BE "IN LIKE," BE IN LOVE

No, this isn't about romantic relationships and dating. What the hell could I offer you on that front that would be worth a damn?

I'm not sure where he got this from (for full transparency, I don't think this can be attributed to him) but my favorite comedian George Carlin (see the chapter on embracing comedy), once said:

The definition of success is:

> *Finding what you love, doing what you love, recognizing that you're good at it, and always getting better at it.*

My advice to you is to have a stake in as many things as possible that goes on in your life. And when you do that, you'll be a more committed person, and possibly happier. I'm not a religious person (I do very much believe in God), but you'll have a life that is more fulfilling, too. I say possibly happier because being a committed person, in general, requires work. But the work is worth it.

Please don't misinterpret this and think I'm trying to tell you to "care" about every little thing in your life and take everything seriously – absolutely not.

What I'm saying is to try your best to not treat the things in your life that matter casually. Because the things in your life that matter – MATTER!

Some of this perhaps I've always had but I've also learned some of this from Steve Jobs. Former students sometimes like to make fun of me and say that I'm obsessed with Steve Jobs and that I constantly use him in innovation and marketing classes. To that, I double down and say forget obsessed, I'm essentially a disciple of Steve Jobs.

Aside from his initial denial of paternity to his daughter Lisa (and I really do mean that; that always bothered me), Steve Jobs is my "messiah."

In the Walter Isaacson biography on Steve Jobs, there's a portion of a chapter that talks about when the Jobs' household had to make a relatively mundane purchase (mundane when you're a multi-billionaire). The story discusses how the entire family had an actual discussion about a washer/dryer at the dinner table, and they landed on buying a Miele. Miele is a great German brand, by the way, that I've been familiar with for some time but can't afford!

When you think about this, that's some commitment to things that many of us wouldn't care about, to this extent. Judge it if you wish, but it's an interesting story that can provide further perspective.

And my advice to you, is to commit to, and be in love with as many things as you can in life. I know it's not always easy, but when you embrace that mindset, you can CONTROL more aspects of your life.

For example, I love my apartment. It's not the biggest apartment in the world, but I bought it and although I pay a hefty mortgage on it, I love it. Whether you rent or own, do your best to live where you want – the difference between living in a house or apartment that you want (and is realistic) vs 'just' taking an apartment as a matter of convenience is BIG.

DO YOU WANT TO LIVE IN A BETTER WORLD, OR SIMPLY HAVE A GOOD LIFE?

I'm asking you to ask yourself this hard question. The distinction is worlds apart. I don't need your answer. You need your answer.

It's an easy question, but most people ignore it. It's one of those fundamental questions about how you see the world. And that's what makes it difficult for most.

Most people are going to answer the latter, whether they know it or not. Maybe at one point in their lives they would have answered the former. But that ship has sailed for them. Sorry to get negative here; it's not my intention.

The positive here is that it's not too late for you if you want the former.

Regardless of your decision, I'm not judging you. The idea here is to get you to think about this, in a deep way. And I'll hit you with some reality here – whatever you decide, you do have to live with your decision. That, I'll need to hold you to.

If you're looking to simply have a good life, that's much easier to achieve. Get a good career, find someone special, maybe have some kids, a house. And don't forget the damn dog. That's it. It doesn't even matter if you're all that successful at it. You can be mildly successful at this grand goal. Be around for 80-90 years if you're lucky, then you'll die, and a handful of people will attend your funeral. Done! Easy-peasy!

But I want to live in a better world. Do you? I always have.

Having a significant other (I hate the term "life partner!"), a few close friends who care about you, a good and rewarding career, a comfortable income level, are all great. But I want to live in a **better** world. I'm not in my twenties anymore, but **I won't give up**.

A healthy dose of bullshit and alcohol is what gets most people through their day. Otherwise, people would need to deal with reality.

Humanity is not ready for that. We haven't evolved to learn how to take care of ourselves and each other, yet.

I think we all need to take responsibility to learn how to evolve. Bullshitting ourselves, is OK, to an extent. But I've been saying for some time that the best type of activism is just focusing on us, as humans.

MOST OF THE WORLD DOESN'T WANT TO LEARN, THEY JUST WANT TO BE ENTERTAINED

The sad truth, which was awful tasting medicine once I realized it, is that most people don't want to learn. They simply want to be entertained.

This is one of the hard truths of the world. This is reality.

The good news, if there is any, is that at least I'm aware of this. And now, so are you. And while it doesn't alleviate all my frustration, it lessens it some.

When I say most people don't want to learn, I'm not talking about attending college. Or in some parts of the world, even primary school.

I'm talking about thinking. Learning how to have better quality thinking, in whatever the issue is. And I'm talking about education, in a broad sense.

The irony, however, is that the most important thing about an undergraduate education is learning how to think. I was taught that as an undergrad, and I've tried to help students understand that throughout the years. For the most part, I have failed.

People typically have little to no interest in learning. Learning new skills, new ways of thinking, new perspectives. If you're reading this book, then you're in the minority.

I used to think, as a dedicated life-long learner, that this was fine. 'Good for me and too bad for those who aren't interested,' I used to say.

But as I've gotten a little older, I no longer have a neutral perspective. I consider this a bad thing. Because we all live in the same world. And if people just put in the slightest amount of a bit more effort to think, the world would be in such a better place.

Have you ever heard of the butterfly effect, which is tied to chaos theory? I learned this taking a philosophy class as an undergrad, and it was fascinating. It's not some fringe theory, and widely accepted by many.

In a nutshell, it's based on the idea that everything is a piece of a connected system. And that small changes that seem unconnected in one part of the system amount to larger changes in other parts of the system. Where the butterfly effect comes into play is the idea that a butterfly flapping its wings somewhere in Europe, for example, ultimately impacts a weather event in Texas.

I'm not trying to prove or disprove this theory with you, that's not what's important. What's interesting is what it suggests.

I think this is due to several factors.

First, learning is **HARD** and **requires** TIME.

Entertainment, which is completely fine in proper doses, is **EASY** and **kills** TIME.

Another reason why the world doesn't want to learn and only entertained is because learning is an unselfish act. Not sure if you've ever really thought of this, but it is.

Even though you are the learner and it's for "you," you don't know when you will use it to your advantage. If you learn something you're seeking, then it's selfish since you want it for a specific reason. If you're entertained, we as humans get the instant gratification we crave - pure selfishness and instant self-interest.

People only learn lessons when something has happened to them directly. No one learns any lessons by observing other people's mistakes...that's not how it works.

FIGURE OUT WHO TO BE IN BED WITH

One of the (at least for me) most unpleasant realities of getting older is that you begin to realize that you need to figure out what you want to be loyal to.

You have several options, but if you're in your mid-twenties and still on the fence, you'll need to pick a side soon.

You can't be loyal to yourself, at least not yet. It just doesn't work that way. People like Larry David are sort of allowed to be loyal to themselves, but that's because Larry David is worth around $1 billion dollars. Assuming you're not, we must accept that we need to play the game.

To what extent you play the game or want to, is up to you. But unfortunately, you need to play the game, in some way.

Here's a bit more bad news for you: playing the game is not just about your career, it also applies to your personal life. Yes. And it kind of sucks that it extends there, too.

And the biggest admission here is that although I finally learned this, I still struggle with it. And my hope is that you don't struggle as much as me.

Being someone who tries to be "balanced" with as many things as you can in your life is an extremely noble yet flawed strategy. You can take a balanced approach to some things, on a case-by-case basis. But when you try to be balanced with all aspects of your life as a general approach, you realize that you, your efforts, and your intentions amount to essentially one thing:

Nothing.

On a tactical level, yes, be as balanced with as many things as you can and try to be level-headed to accept varying perspectives. But ULTIMATELY, you still need to pick a side.

CHAPTER FIVE | EMBRACING STAND-UP COMEDY

CHAPTER PURPOSE:
- Why embracing comedy, if you haven't yet, is pivotal to better understanding yourself and the world.

You might be thinking how and why did a chapter on stand-up comedy make it to one of the twelve life principles?

I take my comedy very seriously.

And if you understand the above statement and don't think of it as an oxymoron or contradiction, you're already halfway there.

If you're not there yet, and haven't yet embraced stand-up comedy, I'm really encouraging you to do so.

The reasons why you should embrace stand-up comedy, and what I want to share with you in this chapter, have to do with the following life characteristics that stand-up comedians can teach us:

- Being vulnerable, which is an essential human trait.

- Showing tremendous courage (high-quality comedians are genuine ARTISTS).

- Being incredibly honest (comedians are brutally honest) with yourself.

- Showing humility and healthy doses of self-deprecation.

I did a chapter in my presentation skills book, *It's Called Presenting, Not Talking Out Loud*, called 'Learning From Comedians.' Since that's a presentation skills book, the point there was a bit different.

But you can learn a LOT about yourself and life by watching and embracing HIGH QUALITY comedians. I say high quality to distinguish from low quality. I completely realize that you may think I'm being judgmental here because the comedians that make you laugh are entirely subjective, right? Yes, you're right. But at the risk of sounding judgmental, just give me a chance to try and explain why there's a distinction between high- and low-quality and what that can mean to you.

Great comedians have a unique talent that you find almost nowhere else in life. The 'greats' eventually make it to mainstream stardom by saying things that most people don't want to hear. Or at least didn't think they wanted to hear. I find that to be a **fascinating paradox**.

Low quality stand-up comedians, in my view, unfortunately are the ones that don't take any risks. They keep it nice and clean and mainstream. When I say 'clean' I don't mean not cursing. I mean offering mild, benign jokes that are little worth your time. Jokes that, quite frankly, you can do without. They don't want to create waves and want to get a career going and keep that career. Maybe they make you laugh, or if not laugh, perhaps chuckle. Maybe. But you can't LEARN anything from them. They are filler. And they are worthless. (OK, maybe I'm being judgmental).

High quality stand-up comedians make you LAUGH like BLOODY HELL but also make you THINK! Great comedians don't ever lie to you. Ever! If you analyze a great comedian, they are purists, in many ways.

Another distinguishable characteristic of high-quality comedians is that their work is truly TIMELESS. And since their work is preserved on video, they don't have to be alive to be entertaining for you to thoroughly enjoy their content. Two stand-up comedians at the top of my list have been dead unfortunately, for some time now.

Please indulge me and let me share with you some high-quality ones. But first, my favorite comedian of all time. And someone who is one of my genuine heroes:

GEORGE CARLIN

I have shown (and introduced) George Carlin to hundreds of students over the past several years. Just to blow off some steam for the last ten minutes of a marketing or innovation class or instructionally in a business communication course.

George Carlin took on major issues, and most of his work, if not all of it, is timeless. Carlin was an entertainer, but he was also a sociologist (and I really mean that). He made you laugh but also made you think. He wasn't afraid to take BIG RISKS. And his content was sometimes on the margins.

In the 1960s, mainstream society cringed at the content he really wanted to do. So, he left the mainstream (what was defined as 'mainstream' at the time). By the 1970s, people began to see his counterculture approach and value. And some of his work made it all the way up to a landmark Supreme Court case with his '7 Words You Can't Say on Television.' By the 1980s and 1990s, he was in the living rooms of millions of Americans.

Today, he's in the hearts and minds of TENS of millions of Americans and others around the world.

A good comedian will shape your general thinking and outlook on life. And that's precisely what Carlin did for me. Carlin shaped my thinking in a very fundamental way when I was in my early twenties, and he's partially responsible for how I see the world. In a way that continues to permeate to this day.

Only **genuine artists** can do that. All artists are entertainers but not all entertainers are artists.

Another thing about great comedians and artists that Carlin taught me is that artists are never satisfied. And if you look at that from the correct perspective, that can be incredibly healthy.

When you see great comedians never being satisfied, that means one thing: <u>growth</u>.

Carlin once said: **'Art is a race, with no finish line.'**

And whether you're a creative person or someone who has a creative streak, in one way or another, you can also live your life in a way where there's always growth, and never a finish line.

This book is for you, but you'll have to forgive me here. I just need to say George Carlin was truly the best.

Take another comedian who I consider a pioneer and legend:

RICHARD PRYOR

Richard Pryor grew up in a brothel (literally) that was run by his grandmother, who would beat him on an almost daily basis. Pryor's mother was a prostitute in the brothel, and his father was her pimp.

Pretty much his entire adult life, even when he made it big, Pryor used to say, "the government says I'm 'illegitimate' and all of my life people have been saying 'I'm no good'." His rise to the top was not only about his talent as a comedian; he was also a sociologist, and in the 1960s and 1970s, probably did more for the relationship between whites and blacks than most people of his time.

Let me be clear, I'm NOT promoting drug use at all. But great comedians are also vulnerable, and they're not afraid to share their vulnerabilities, whatever they are, with the world. Both Carlin and Pryor were big time drug users during the peak of the careers.

I believe George Carlin did an interview sometime in the 1980s with Johnny Carson or someone, where he said: 'In the 1970s, I snorted half of Colombia. And Richard Pryor snorted the other half.'

And Richard Pryor once said in an interview: 'I don't like cocaine, I love it.'

It's true that Richard Pryor's cocaine dealer at one point wouldn't sell him anymore, out of concern for his well-being.

When you're a multi-millionaire celebrity and even your drug dealer won't sell you any more drugs? Wow! Just wow.

When Richard Pryor was admitted to a burn trauma unit in the early 1980s, there was a lot of speculation as to what happened. Many, at first, thought there was an accidental fire in his home. After many months of rehabilitation, Pryor finally did an interview where he was asked what happened. He simply said, 'I tried to kill myself, next question.'

If that's not brutal honesty, I don't know what is. Great comedians are a special breed.

If you haven't yet made stand-up comedy a PERMANENT part of your life, in the same way that many people live and breathe sports, I highly suggest you start now.

Your life will be richer, more dimensional, and more complex. I said complex, not complicated. Complexity is a good thing ☺.

CHAPTER SIX | MOST THINGS IN LIFE BOIL DOWN TO MONEY

CHAPTER PURPOSE:
- Whether you like it or not, the reality is that most motivations in the world boil down to money.

Since there's so much that can be said here, this is one of those topics that I'll try and keep succinct. I'll provide some commentary but use examples, for the most part.

When I was in my twenties, this used to make me quite angry. It still does, but not as much. I've learned to accept it, unwittingly.

And if it makes you angry, I'm with you on this. You know how you hear people older than you, maybe even a parent, say essentially the same thing but you've always sort of felt they were exaggerating, being negative, or cynical? Well, they're right on this.

Unfortunately, most things in life boil down to money.

The reason why I'm sharing this is not to be the messenger of bad news. Instead, it's to prepare you and help you better understand SO MANY things you observe and why they happen.

Here are a few examples that, admittedly, when I was younger, I genuinely didn't understand (if you already knew these examples, you're a better person than me).

Example 1:
In many suburbs across the United States, one thing you'll notice is that the public high school system that serves that district is quite good. It has a solid reputation, has very good, caring teachers, and perhaps has won various state and federal awards in the field of public education.

And so, you might think (especially if you're a product of the public elementary and high school system like me), this is great. A high school that has strong leadership and a high degree of caring and commitment to students and education.

Nope.

While the above might be true about the high school (and if you're thinking, that's what counts at the end of the day, OK) but you need to understand why.

The reason for this is because the suburbs of America are designed mainly for families. And when young parents or young couples who are planning to be parents buy a home, they're thinking about how good the public school system in the district is, to consider sending their kids there.

A good public school system means that there is high demand to live in that town. And that means the value (and prices) of homes in that area go up. And that means more tax revenue can be assessed.

That's all it is folks. The "kids" and their education are an afterthought. It's the MONEY that counts. Never let anyone lie to you and tell you differently.

Example 2:
This is an example where the money no longer matters. But **still** revolves around money.

Up until a few years ago (as of this writing) pharmacy chains such as Duane Reade/Walgreens, CVS, etc. sold cigarettes. I remember when the local pharmacy store in my hometown in New Jersey used to also sell liquor, which I always thought was strange.

All these chains keep publicly providing essentially the same (bullshit) statement. I'm just paraphrasing here but it goes something along the lines of:

We've decided to no longer sell tobacco products, in line with our mission to help our customers live more active and healthy lives.

Holy Jesus! Duane Reade and CVS genuinely care about your health? **WOW!** I swear, these are the sweetest, kindest people on earth. What saints these people are!

But how about telling the **truth**? The truth is that since less Americans smoke tobacco products than they historically used to, these categories have shrunken below a threshold where the revenue and product simply doesn't matter anymore. They can discontinue these categories with essentially no impact to their business.

Believe me, if more people continued to smoke cigarettes, these pharmacy chains would continue to sell them. And privately, they probably wouldn't not care whether you put a cigarette in your mouth or up your ass. If you kept buying them.

Example 3:
When Mike Bloomberg became mayor of New York City in the early 2000s, one of his first missions was to ban cigarette smoking in bars. My understanding is that Bloomberg was a smoker for approximately 30 years before quitting, and he understood first-hand the dangers of smoking.

This was before the days of vaping, and although by the early 2000s smoking had declined, it was still a prevalent problem in American society.

So many people were up in arms over this, and a whole range of people – from decently intelligent to your typical, average moron – had an opinion on this.

They said Bloomberg didn't understand New York or New Yorkers. They said he was going to destroy the bar and restaurant business in New York City. They said he was crazy.

The law went into effect and guess what happened?

The opposite.

Not only did the bar business survive, but it also thrived. Regardless of where your politics falls when Bloomberg was mayor, Mike Bloomberg is a businessman and a self-made billionaire worth somewhere around $90 billion, as of this writing.

Bloomberg understood that by banning smoking in bars, people who typically didn't go to bars because of the cigarette smoke would probably start going. And he was right. It's marketing – it's target markets. It's where the numbers fall in terms of smokers vs. non-smokers (non-smokers were already the majority by the early 2000s). And marrying that with the number of people who would otherwise spend more time in bars and restaurants, if it wasn't for the smoking.

While banning smoking in bars was important to him on a personal level, do you think he was going to jeopardize an entire sector of New York's economy? Do you think he needs a lecture on the basics of how the economy works? He's not stupid.

Example 4:
Let me be clear, I don't in any way dismiss the seriousness of this issue. If anything, this should support the nature of it.

In the modern world, especially in the United States, instances of sexual harassment in the workplace happen often, unfortunately. And while I don't have the exact statistics (and I don't need them for the purposes of this), the majority of those who are accused of sexual harassment are terminated from their jobs.

To the victims, this might feel as though there is some degree of justice that's taken place (might). And if so, I'm not suggesting that there wasn't any justice, nor am I suggesting that the company wasn't sensitive to the matter and all the facts surrounding it. And I'm sincere when I say I respect the severity of how the victims of sexual harassment situations made them feel.

At the same time, I need to tell you the truth. The company may have some sincere sentiment towards the victim, but that is NOT why they were rather swift and efficient with their investigation process, and how they rather swiftly terminated the individual who was accused.

Not one bit. And NEVER for one second in your life think that the company's actions were for the victim. The company moved swiftly because of one simple reason: they don't want the victim to sue the company.

I'm not a lawyer, and labor laws evolve (of course). I can't speak to all the complexities. But I can tell you that that's why the company acted the way they did.

It's for the company, not the victim. The company can say: 'We didn't know about this prior, we learned of it, conducted an investigation, and promptly acted.'

That keeps them relatively safe. Some companies, of course, lie. They may have known about the general behavior, or they may have a company culture that condones the behavior. But they will lie. It's as simple as that.

It's about money. In this case, not having to (hopefully) deal with a lawsuit between the victim and the company.

If the company, through their investigation, felt there wasn't quite enough there. And that if they were to terminate the accused, they can sue the company, then the accused wouldn't be terminated. Perhaps internal training, redirection of work duties, etc., would happen.

Again, it's about money.

And how can I ignore one of biggest areas where you see this on an almost daily basis:

CORPORATE SPONSORSHIPS

I don't think this requires much explanation. Actually, let's have a little 'fun' with this one. There's at least one good thing that can come out of this book coming out later than expected.

In general, as you know, every corporate sponsor that either says or does something that causes general backlash is booted. Companies love to say, as though they're on autopilot, that the individual's behavior is 'inconsistent with our values.'

Is the behavior inconsistent with the company's values? Maybe it is and maybe it isn't. We don't know. Do you have the ability and time to interview everyone at the company, or at least all the executives of the company?

But what we do know (for certain) is that the behavior is INCONSISTENT WITH SALES GOALS. That's the only damn thing that's inconsistent.

Bud Light's recent case is an interesting one; it goes in the reverse but still supports my point. In case you don't know, in early 2023 Bud Light (beer) partnered with transgender influence Dylan Mulvaney. The director of marketing for Bud Light felt that the brand was getting stale and needed new life.

Dylan Mulvaney posted one video on social media saying:

"This month I celebrated my day 365 of womanhood, and bud light sent me possibly the best gift ever, a can with my face on it."

This started a backlash that spun in an interesting way (I acknowledge the political aspects of this) but let's stick with the business aspects. Because they're all intertwined.

Sales of Bud Light began to plummet and have been plummeting for the past four weeks as of this writing.

A few days after the backlash began, the director of marketing along with the vice president of marketing took a 'leave of absence.'

The CEO of Anheuser-Busch said:

"We never intended to be part of a discussion that divides people," Anheuser-Busch CEO Brendan Whitworth said. "We are in the business of bringing people together over a beer."

It didn't matter. Sales continue to plummet. Bud Light is now offering free cases of beer to their wholesale distributors, to try and shore up an all-out implosion of the brand.

I'm genuinely being neutral here, and I hope you understand that. But what happened when celebrities like Kid Rock as well as others calling for a boycott to the brand? The company didn't subscribe to the typical 'these comments are inconsistent with our values.'

Well, the opposite in this case, and different, but same. It's about the money.

Whenever you're examining an issue, train your mind to ALWAYS think about the financial implications. It doesn't mean you have to become cynical (although some degree of cynicism is healthy), I'm asking you to train your mind in this manner because it's the smart and appropriate way to think.

Almost every aspect of life in the modern world has a financial implication that will be the driving force of whatever decision is made.

I promise you – this is how it works.

Ladies and gentlemen, welcome to the real world!

Hallelujah and holy shit!

CHAPTER SEVEN | RELAX, ALMOST EVERYONE PANDERS TO THEIR BASE

CHAPTER PURPOSE:
1. To have the ability to see beyond the NONSENSE of most companies and certain people.
2. To have a better perspective on why most companies and certain people say what they say, and when they conveniently say it.

One thing that many young people can't necessarily yet see is how a lot of the behavior of corporations, organizations, and certain individuals boils down to one simple thing:

The Base.

I promised you a book that is usable, so I'm going to share various examples that are not philosophical, and hopefully, relatable.

Let me start with this. Every now and again, once the holidays are in full swing (or maybe every year), the following scenario comes up:

During the holiday season, Starbucks' cups say, 'Happy Holidays,' 'Season's Greetings,' etc.

Some people in the Christian community don't appreciate why Starbucks doesn't write 'Merry Christmas.'

At the same time, Wal-Mart's greeters are trained to say 'Merry Christmas' to their guests.

Some people in the Jewish and Muslim community don't appreciate why Wal-Mart doesn't say 'Happy Holidays' or 'Season's Greetings.'

Then there's all this chatter on social media, and people begin fighting with one another over really nothing.

Want the truth? Starbucks has a customer base that is multi-cultural, and Starbucks' customers come from many religions, ethnicities, etc.

Wal-Mart's core customer, which has many Hispanic customers as well as other ethnicities – are mainly members of the Christian faith.

Why the hell would you risk saying 'Merry Christmas' to Jewish people and Muslims, and alienate Christians by offering a diluted 'Happy Holidays?'

These companies have BUSINESSES TO PROTECT. They are not stupid. They know what they're doing.

That's all it is folks. Done! That's why these two companies do what they do. There's nothing else going on here. It's genuinely as simple as that.

Now, there are things that I wish I could tell you for the next example, but unfortunately, I can't tell you everything (and I'm sincerely sorry for that). But...

Almost all (almost) university and college presidents have 100% support for DREAMERS (DACA). And they go out of their way (they really do, sometimes in an unnecessary way) to also state, in no uncertain terms, that no student's status will ever be reviewed or questioned.

Why?

Because right now DREAMERS are of college age or college-bound age.

DREAMERS are a good portion of their **customers**. It's part of their **base!**

I have experience working in many different types of colleges and universities: private, private (prestigious), public, public (prestigious), faith-based, etc.

Now let me share another example from my industry, corporate retail. When Ron Johnson, the former CEO of JC Penney, came and went with an awful 18-month tenure. For us in the retail sector, some of us saw the problems from the start.

Ron Johnson wanted to transform an ailing and aging retailer – nothing wrong there.

In a nutshell, he cleaned up the store aesthetics (especially in the home area), took away heavy discounting, created 'everyday fair and square pricing,' and discontinued the catalog.

All these changes resulted in something: the core JC Penney customer was alienated, and no one was really in the stores anymore – literally. Johnson basically told the JC Penney customer to "go to hell." And that's OK in business if you have a new customer to replace them. But he didn't. So, what happened? He alienated the core customer that was loyal to the store, for right or wrong reasons. **He alienated the base.**

Another example, and this one I can freely tell you. Although I'm an Apple fan, I'm more of a Steve Jobs fan, not a Tim Cook fan. Tim Cook is a capable operator, but he knows nothing about product (I'm a product guy, by training) and that angers me tremendously. He needs to go back to having his old job as COO, not CEO.

Anyway (thanks for letting me vent there a bit), but do you remember the unfortunate terrorist attack in

2015 in southern California? Where the FBI went to Apple, to open the dead terrorists iPhone 5C, and Apple said no.

The FBI said that this person KILLED several people and injured many. And they just needed to get into ONE phone.

Apple still said no. And shame on Apple for doing that. And I guess good for the person who went to the FBI and opened the iPhone for them – I'm sure he was paid handsomely but the sum was never disclosed.

Tim Cook said on several occasions, some long-winded nonsense that was allegedly rooted in privacy and the tenets of privacy and that our democracy is partially built on privacy, etc. It all sounded good to the UNTRAINED ear.

100% Grade-A, USDA-Certified BULLSHIT!

Pure Hogwash!

The reason why Apple refused is because they didn't want to set a precedent. Because I'm sorry to say but a lot (not all, but a lot) of people, at least in this country, and other parts of the world – SEXT. (You know, texting sexual things). They send lots of dirty messages and dirty pictures.

Imagine if you heard that Apple was opening an iPhone for law enforcement. You might drop everything and go and get a Samsung Galaxy instead, like yesterday! No SERIOUSLY...that's not a joke! A good amount of people would jump ship.

How dare Apple get in the way of you sexting the person you're having an affair with! The nerve of those folks in Cupertino!

Apple was simply pandering to their base. They were, as in the other examples, PROTECTING THEIR BUSINESS.

It's much ado about nothing. And once again, it's as simple as that.

Let me also balance this out with an example from politics. Politicians are experts at this, but do you remember when Mike Bloomberg, former New York City Mayor and billionaire businessman had that brief 2020 presidential run? If you don't remember, it's OK, it lasted a whole five minutes.

Anyway, Mike Bloomberg went to the biggest black church in Harlem to apologize to black people for his stop-and-frisk policing policies while he was a three-term mayor.

When he was mayor, people would often ask him why he had his police department conduct most stop-and-frisk procedures in black-majority neighborhoods in Brooklyn and the Bronx? His answer was simple: He said, 'because that's where the criminals are.'

But once he started running for president, he quickly changed his tune. Again, his presidential campaign lasted an entire five minutes, pretty much. But why did he go to a major black church in Harlem? He was hoping for some black votes, damnit!

Or as some white politicians, like John F. Kennedy used to call it – the negro vote.

Let me end with one hypothetical, light-hearted example. Let's say there was a Muslim who owned a lemonade stand (let's keep it simple) in a predominantly Jewish neighborhood where most of the customers were Jewish. I promise you that each morning they would offer an enthusiastic, 'Shalom!'

And if the lemonade stand owner was Jewish in a predominantly Muslim neighborhood with mostly Muslim customers, every morning they would offer a hearty, 'Salam Aleichem!'

THERE ARE TWO TYPES OF VICIOUS LIES IN THE WORLD

This is not about the difference between 'real' lies and 'white' lies. I think we learn that at around age five and I wouldn't insult your intelligence that way.

This chapter is about another type of vicious, hurtful lie. And it happens all the time. It's very sinister because it's the type of lie that doesn't exist.

Sometimes people will say this type of lie is not a lie but at best, it's misleading.

NO, IT'S A LIE. A HEINOUS, VICIOUS, BONA FIDE LIE. Never forget that.

To me, it's the most evil type of lie. Worse than your "typical" lie.

The media lies like this at its very fundamental core. It couldn't exist without this lie. Let me explain.

Every major media organization and organization that has journalism at its core will generally take a very strong stance against impropriety of almost any kind.

Take this as just one of many examples: Think of when famous (now disgraced) journalist Brian Williams, who was demoted in 2015 when an internal investigation found that while reporting on the Iraq war in 2003, he lied when he said he was in a Chinook helicopter with special forces. He was lucky he wasn't fired.

When these types of issues come about, news organizations go out of their way to inform the public that journalistic integrity is the very pinnacle (or insert some other fancy sounding word) of what they do. And that PUBLIC TRUST is more important than anything.

Sounds pretty good, especially to young people, right? Reminds you that a few things in life, such as justice and fairness are at play...on some level, yes?

OK, that's NOT a classic lie. But they're not telling you the truth. And when you don't tell people the truth on either matters of significant importance or organizations that have great societal influence, it is a HEINOUS lie.

What they're not telling you is that they're not interested in the principles of fair play and honesty. They could care less, at least as concepts. They need to adhere to those principles on a tactical level.

All media organizations (and it's not just politics and that's why I'm saying all media organizations, not just news organizations) must come at some reporting angle, or perspective. When a media organization begins to develop themselves into a brand, the only way to do that is develop an audience. And the audience is their lifeline since a developed audience means a predictable audience. And that means that more predictable advertising revenue can be generated.

Sure, opinion pieces are the exception, but that's why they are always qualified by 'the opinions in this piece don't necessarily reflect the opinions of this organization,' etc. And by the way, opinion pieces are HIGHLY selective and edited anyway. You cannot write an opinion piece for CNN if there's too much truth about the Democrat party. And you cannot write an opinion piece for Fox News if there's too much truth about the Republican party. Opinion pieces are like when a lawyer does a little bit of pro bono work each year. It's charity. It's goodwill. CNN and Fox News will let you say a 'little' but only if it doesn't piss off their audience much.

The unfortunate truth about how the modern world works is that organizations will only talk about things such as 'truth, honor, integrity,' etc. when they get caught, and the financial consequences and backlash will be worse than continuing to toe the line.

Otherwise, it's business as usual. Under normal business conditions, 'truth, honor, and integrity' are cute novelties that are laughed at by senior management.

As I said folks, most people are simply pandering to their base or pandering to a base that they want. That's all it is.

MOST ORGANIZATIONS WILL NEVER TELL YOUNG PEOPLE THIS

In some ways, this is the most important section of the book. And, sometimes the most important things are the ones that don't seem it.

One of the sincerest things I need to share with you is how to manage various concerns/crises/issues in your life. Especially when you're young.

Because when you're young, many people will try (try) to take advantage of you.

And I will be GODDAMNED if I didn't tell you what I need to here – so that you can navigate more successfully.

When you've been wronged in some way and have been working hard to stick up for your rights or what is owed you (which is a hard task in and of itself and you have a lot of courage for initiating the process – I know), you're most likely dealing with powerful organizations. And it's a powerful organization vs. you, the little guy. Or little gal – sorry ladies. And those powerful organizations want to crush you. Like a little bug. So, you can go away.

Let's say you decide to sue a former employer for unpaid wages. And you want to sue them yourself and not hire a lawyer. You have that right in the United States, in general (not sure about certain states or other countries).

Your former company has a powerful law firm on retainer for precisely these types of things.

Friendly reminder: they want to crush you like a bug. They want to destroy you like the little PISS ANT that they think you are.

There will be times in the process where you'll be in a lull. And you'll feel as though you're not continuing to get traction.

And because you're just one person, it can get tough when you're in that lull. The attorney assigned is not answering your emails – they were but now they've gone MIA (because they're playing games with you, by the way). And one of the top tools that lawyers unfortunately have at their disposal is to try and **beat the clock**. And simply manipulate the concept of time with you.

What are your options? Sending the judge a letter? Probably not.

Perhaps you can go to the American Bar Association or similar association at the state level and file a complaint. You have that option but usually – those types of organizations take complaints based on ethical concerns. Now, whether you feel that an attorney playing games with you is unethical or not – you'll need to decide, and I won't ever tell you what to think, only help you how to think.

You may clearly see on their website that the complaint needs to be an ethical one of sorts. And as a young person, you may not move forward.

So, here's my advice: MOVE FORWARD.

The name of the game here, and the game you need to learn and play, is to get attention.

That's the goal. Do you genuinely think there is an ethical scandal here? Maybe not. But if you're now being ignored, you need to do something to get un-ignored.

If the attorney for the defense and their firm, in general, receive a complaint filed by you by the American Bar Association, the attorney will now be in touch with you.

I promise this will work 95% of the time.

What's the point here, and how to we wrap this up? The point here is that you need to break certain 'rules,' from time-to-time.

Do NOT break the law. I don't want you to do something in haste and wind up with a NEW court date – the kind where you're the defense and the prosecutor is against you. That you don't want.

Powerful corporations want you to simply go away. Their modus operandi is to get you to go away, to give up. Whatever the issue is – don't let them cast you aside.

And that, as they say, is THAT!

CHAPTER EIGHT | POWER, PERSUASION, AND CHANGE

CHAPTER PURPOSE:
1. To help, to some extent, the basics of power structures.
2. To offer a general basis for how to influence and persuade people.

I wanted to include a chapter on power and persuasion since I think it's something that's incredibly important to young people, and misunderstood, to an extent.

Young people have self-interest in the concept of power. One reason has to do with many young people wanting to see change.

Power sometimes is viewed as someone holding some type of role or title, and therefore having 'power.' But that really doesn't help answer what power is and begs the question. Power isn't so much about someone's role – although that may play some part.

An easy definition of power is an individual that is in possession of, or in charge of, something that you want.

A hiring manager has power over the open position since they will ultimately make the decision who gets the job. A college instructor holds temporary power over students in a course since they are responsible for assigning the final course grades and have some discretion over which students ultimately receive a good grade. Once the semester is over (assuming the student doesn't have the same instructor again), that power the instructor had been completely gone.

But if you were a college student and someone pointed out an instructor that didn't even teach at your school, you wouldn't consider them as having any power, right? And there can also be people who have power over something but no role. Such as someone who has information that can be used against someone else if they don't get what they want.

So, it's not so much about the role but more about what the person possesses that someone else needs or wants.

One of the most important things to understand about power in relation to change is that power is not something that people are interested in giving up. Why would you give up power unless you have to? Or are forced to?

WHY CHANGE IS SO SLOW

I'm willing to bet that one of the most frustrating issues you come across as a young person is why change takes so long, yes? I feel confident about this because it's exactly how I felt when I was in my twenties. And it's how most young people feel, universally.

I'm not an expert on this topic, and I don't have all the answers on this. But I have *some* of the answers. And based on the pragmatic nature of this book, I'm hoping having at least some of the answers is enough.

The first issue I'll say, in all sincerity, is that one of the fundamental reasons why change takes so long is because we as humans think too highly of ourselves. We really do.

While the human brain is fascinating on some levels, on other levels, not so much.

I'm not a psychologist or psychiatrist, but I've done some studying on this, asked some licensed psychiatrists, along with many years of observation.

Yes, you've already heard millions of times, people resist change. Because we don't like the unknown. Even young people – many of which want change – aren't necessarily comfortable with changes in their own lives, per se. Right? Seriously, think about it for a second. So, if you also resist change, why do you "demand" change from others? (that's a rhetorical question and I'm not putting you in a defensive position).

I think, from a more sociological level, humans truly need baby steps. Some of us may need more and some less. But we all need to be spoon fed change. We need to get introduced to it, begin to get used to it, and gradually accept it. It's a process.

I'm going to use some examples here that I hope won't offend anyone, but I think work.

In the United States, unfortunately we have a history of black Americans as slaves. Then white Americans for a very long time called blacks the n-word to their face. Then whites referred to blacks the n-word behind their back. And now, whites have begun to realize that there have been fundamental, systemic obstacles that blacks have faced for over a century.

Of course, race is the most complex issue the United States will continue to have, but for the country to get to at least this level, took time. I don't think whites could go from owning blacks as slaves to now being in general alignment on systemic race issues that are challenging to blacks. That's simply far too much of a leap of faith.

KNOWING THE OPPOSING PERSPECTIVE IS CRITICAL TO WINNING

To effectively persuade people or groups on any topic to advance your cause, you need to also understand how the opposition feels.

Probably the most important thing I learned as an undergrad studying sociology, aside from the topics themselves, is that to effectively advance my perspective and point of view, I needed to make sure I understood the opposition. I mean, really understand it. It doesn't matter if you strongly disagree with the opposition; you need to understand why the opposition feels the way they do.

Frist, to tackle the obvious, you won't be able to effectively take a position if you're ignorant of the opposing viewpoint.

- How can you advocate for abortion rights if you don't fully understand what makes people opposed to it?

- How can you argue for the abolishment of the death penalty if you don't understand why there are those who are in favor of it?

- How can you oppose climate change if you aren't familiar enough with the reasons why climate change activists strongly advocate on its impact?

You'd be surprised how many middle-aged and older people don't seem to understand this.

They simply reject whatever it is they want to reject without even knowing what they're fully objecting to.

Another way to describe the above people is this way: they are your typical, everyday moron, on both sides of the political aisle.

To persuade, one of the keys is to anticipate the objections BECAUSE the people with the best persuasion skills know how to spin their arguments in a way that doesn't make the opposition feel so opposed.

Let me say that again in a different way. First, you don't need to persuade people who already agree with you, right? They are already on your side. Therefore, you're trying to persuade the naysayers. The best way to do that is to show the opposition that they aren't as opposed as they may think. That's a key strategy that many people aren't aware of.

When you can convince the opposition that you're not as far apart as it may seem, persuading others becomes a lot easier. There isn't nearly as much heavy lifting.

The differences between the opposition and you begin to not seem that far apart.

And you know how all modern cars, starting sometime in the 90s have 'Objects in mirror may be closer than they appear?'

Well, the similarities between you and the opposition can also be closer than they appear, when you can effectively persuade people.

Remember, persuasion doesn't mean FIGHT. Persuasion implies you want to get others who don't currently agree with you, on your side.

You can't do that unless you not only understand their points of view BUT you also need to 'give' them something.

You need to provide the opposition with some OWNERSHIP in the issue. Because when people who don't agree with you feel completely left out, they'll further oppose you and your viewpoints.

Bring the opposition closer to you. I promise; you might be a bit surprised with the results.

WHY THINGS GET MORE BLACK AND WHITE AS YOU GET OLDER

One of the things that young people hate is when older people come across as 'black and white.' It kind of drives you crazy to think that your parents, relatives, and other people older than you are close-minded.

Because you like to think in shades of gray and are happy that you're no longer a kid. And that you embrace gray.

Am I right?

I **totally** get how you feel. I used to feel people who thought in black and white terms and didn't embrace the "gray" in life were ignorant, lazy, and perhaps sometimes even unintelligent (ok, let's just use the word "stupid").

Ok, there are people who think in black and white due to some of the above. But as I now better understand why that happens as you get older. Because I know see it sometimes happening to me. Not always, but sometimes.

There are a few reasons why I think this starts to happen:

- As you get older, you get more life experience. Experience is an accumulation of various things that manifests itself into knowledge, insight, perspective, etc.

- And part of gaining more experience means that in cases where you've already been through the same, or very similar experience, you are certain that you'll know the outcome.

- And it's that probability of knowing the outcome, that allows you to make a prediction fast without the need to think about it, and consider various alternatives, etc.

- In some ways, it's not being closed-minded at all. Due to more experience, the mind can go through calculations more quickly, which to younger people with less experience, comes across as though you're too quick to draw a conclusion.

As you gain more experience, the world becomes smaller. That doesn't mean you should ever stop learning. I (sincerely) consider myself a student of life and have every intention to continue to learn for the rest of my life. But in some ways, the world does get smaller.

When you start your very first 'real' job out of college, assuming you're going to stay in that industry your entire career, you're a blank slate. And that's not a criticism; it's just normal. But as time goes on and you learn more, you learn not only more about your job. You learn more about the industry, the competitors, etc. And things get smaller.

If you've dated several TYPES of people, then you're probably going to be able to tell what may happen in certain situations with certain types of people. Fair? It really sort of works the same way.

What often happens in the mind of someone young when being presented with a situation probably looks something like this:

- Situation
- Options
- Concerns
- Consequences
- Outcome/Opinion

What often happens in the mind of someone older with more experience probably looks a little more like this:

- Situation
- Consequences
- Concerns
- Options
- Outcome/Opinion

As you can see, the parts in the middle of each are rearranged. It will happen to you too (which I don't see as a bad thing, per se). As you gain more experience with things that are the same as before, or similar, you'll be able to digest the situation faster and your motivation will most likely be governed by understanding the consequences that immediately follow.

There's another reason why things tend to get more black and white, and the shades of gray go away after time.

In many aspects of one's life, things are ultimately binary. In other words, either something is going to happen, or it's not.

And I know that this also is sometimes unsettling to young people. But it's true. Either something is going to happen, or it won't.

- You're doing your best and going through that brutal job interview process with multiple rounds because you want to work in that company starting next month.

- You're going to figure out how to get the money to pay for your child's education, so s/he doesn't need to drop out, since you just unfortunately lost your job.

- You're going to work super hard for the next two years because you want to save enough of a down payment to buy your first house or apartment.

- You've decided to put your best effort into your relationship with your significant other, since you want to make the relationship work.

I hope this makes sense. Ultimately, things are going to happen, or they won't. And as you get older, due to better (and more) experience, you'll go about understanding and executing through decisions in a more efficient way. Due to a better understanding of the big picture.

CHAPTER NINE | LIKABILITY

CHAPTER PURPOSE:
1. Being liked is essential to your success.
2. Being right is not as important as being liked.

Each of us know people who told us, at some time in our lives: You don't need to have everyone like you; you just need them to respect you.

They are so unbelievably wrong. Or at least (partially) unbelievably wrong.

Some of you may already be very well-versed in this, but many of us need to be exposed to the concept of likability, and its importance.

The degree to which you are liked will determine, to a strong extent, how successful you'll be in your professional and personal life.

It sometimes (sometimes too often) means that those who are very politically savvy will win. Even when they don't deserve to.

I know – that kind of sucks, right? If that bothers you, well, it's always bothered me. But I've had to LEARN TO ACCEPT this and embrace it. And I suggest you do, too.

As you go through your career, people who are in positions of authority/hiring will select you for jobs or special projects (that can really put your career on a nice path) based on your personality more than your skills.

Your skills matter – a lot. But when it comes to a balancing act, some skills and a lot of likability will almost always beat lots of skills and low likability.

When you're growing up, many people tell you something that goes like this:

You don't need everyone to like you, as long as most people respect you.

Well, I'd like to somewhat challenge that. Because I've learned that's only half right.

It's great to be respected, sure. But I have to say, I think likability needs to be weighed just as equally.

Likability is essential to your success in life.

Let me repeat:

Likability is essential to your success in life.

There are so many people who have lots of talent, but not many people like them. And that directly impacts their ability to succeed in whatever they are doing, whether it's in life in general. Or a project. Or anything in between.

When people like you, they are so much more receptive to your ideas and input. Because they like you, they want to hear from you. They're probably hoping to hear from you. When you are liked:

- You get more attention from people
- Things, in general, are SO MUCH easier
- You can accomplish goals faster
- You'll have far more opportunities
- You may have more leadership opportunities
- You will have more general happiness and satisfaction

Notice I'm not talking about friendships – I think that's a given. No need to even bother with that.

One of the things many people make a mistake with is thinking that if they are right, that's what ultimately matters.

Wrong.

You can be certainly <u>right</u> in whatever it is you're talking about/advocating. You can be actually and technically, correct. But sadly, often that doesn't matter.

How many times have you heard about people who were right, in hindsight, but it still didn't matter? A lot! Whether they should've gotten the job, the promotion, the raise, etc.

But it doesn't matter. Time sometimes runs out. The moment passed. They should've gotten the job, etc. But they didn't.

When people don't like you, it's the opposite – literally. It becomes very difficult to offer suggestions, input, etc., and most importantly – **when people don't like you, they don't trust you.**

When people don't like you, but you still have a job to do (and people know that), it's so much more heavy lifting. Really.

The reason why it's so much harder is because if you're not liked, every time you have something to say, the listener(s) first need to filter past your personality and then they MAY listen.

People who are mature will listen a little easier and be a bit fairer. But in general, it's just an all-around losing proposition. Like I said, a lot of unnecessary heavy lifting.

I don't have a degree in psychology, so I'm sure that some people can provide all the intricate conditions, precursors, theories, whatever...as to why this is true. But the reasons and theories don't matter.

I'm here to help you with real-world results.

I won't get into all the forms that likability comes in. I'd rather focus on how to be likable and be cognizant of it.

Some people have dynamic personalities. They just have a good, general disposition and are mostly positive and upbeat. I have some of this but wish I had more of this quality.

You might simply be the easy-going type of person who is easy to talk to, maybe funny, and as some people sometimes say, they "like your face."

One of the keys to be likable in your career is to generally be agreeable. If you're thinking that this sounds like being 'political,' yes, you're exactly right!

When I was younger, being political wasn't something that I wanted to embrace. There seems to be a fakeness to it, which there is. But it doesn't have to be completely fake. And furthermore, it's the way of the world.

Being agreeable doesn't necessarily mean you have to "kiss ass" all the time (maybe sometimes, though) and it also doesn't mean you can't offer your thoughts and viewpoints. Nor does it mean you can't disagree on certain things.

However, being agreeable does mean that in general, you're on the same page as everyone else, you're a team player, you're supportive, and that you're PREDICATABLE.

In the business world, management likes people who are predictable, since they have a good sense that you will support the overall position of the company, or team, etc. And that translates into being likable.

Another way to be likable is to simply be **useful**. Become the person that (in whatever context it makes sense) is as indispensable as possible. Yes, we're all replaceable. But if you become the person that's willing to do things that others seem to not want to do, it sometimes works. When I say doing things that others don't want to do, I don't mean doing anything immoral. Nor do I mean scrubbing the toilets (not that there's anything wrong with that).

Here's an example of what I mean. For about five years, I taught at a university where I got along with the chair of the marketing department more than people may think, but she had her quirks. (Some of her quirks are like mine, and partly why we generally saw eye-to-eye, at the end of the day.)

While she may not want to admit it, a good part of the reason I was there for a while has nothing to do with me being (hopefully) a solid adjunct marketing instructor.

Maybe she feels that way a little, but at best, that might be 20% of why I was there. The main reason I was there for a while was because I was useful to her. I taught the marketing courses at the times no one else wanted to. And this is a tight-knit school where many students are in the same courses each semester, based on major. I also got courses where she taught the same students last semester, and frankly she didn't want to deal with those students again. So, she gave the course(s) to me.

I do believe the chair and a few other administrators liked me, so that's not the issue. But I was liked not for my ability, experience, dedication, skills, or hard work – for the most part.

I was liked **because I had a use**, for a time. And that's just unfortunately the truth.

I mentioned that the second objective in this chapter is about accepting that being right is not as important as being liked. And that's another truth that you'll need to accept, even if it's a hard pill to swallow.

As I said in the introduction, I wrote this book for you and not to talk about me. But I must admit: Over the years, I've had a lot of pointless points.

If you don't know Billy Joel's song, 'Angry Young Man,' listen to it on the internet. That song was truly written for guys like me. Every word of that song was me when I was in my 20s. Every damn word. It's so accurate that it's frightening.

If you have a personality like mine, that's generally rooted in principles, I want to share some advice that may help you not be disappointed as often as you otherwise would.

Let me just make one quick distinction. When I say a personality rooted in principles, I'm not suggesting that most people don't have general morals. I mean having a personality that's rooted in principles – in a more stubborn way.

One of the things I've had to learn over the years is that whether I like it or not (and I still don't), sometimes, even though I know I'm right, I need to sacrifice being right for the sake of something bigger. That 'something bigger' is a friendship, relationship, etc.

If you're like me, it sucks. It's just one of those things in life that sucks. Because some things in life suck.

They don't get better. They just suck – from start to end. Did I say they suck?

There have been times, earlier in my life, where I've known I'm right. But my position wasn't the popular one. And I've lost in those cases. Because when you're right but on an island by yourself, you are usually wrong – unfortunately.

And most of the time, there's no solace in people realizing that you were right, sometime later in the future. Because in most situations, people realizing that you were right "all along" is far too late for anything good to come out of it, for you. And that's what it's about. And there's nothing wrong with being selfish in this regard.

Whatever you do in your life, especially if you're that determined crusader, make sure that people like you along the way. Once you make it to the very top, then you can tell everyone that you're right and they're wrong.

But you need people to like you. You need people to support you. There's no other way.

CHAPTER TEN | CORPORATE CULTURE AND POLITICS

CHAPTER PURPOSE:
1. Understanding why corporate politics and 'playing the game' is important.
2. Understanding the real definition of 'politics' and how to benefit.

Whether you're still in school or now in your first few years of your career, you've already heard how important corporate culture is, I'm sure. And how important being able to mesh with a culture is. And why you were a great candidate but didn't get the job because the hiring manager didn't think you'd 'fit the culture.'

All of this is so incredibly true.

Here's the break-down. This way, you're not simply told this one million times but can better understand it. And the more you understand it, the more you can make it work for you.

Let me also share that since I also teach as my second career, I've learned over the past few years how important corporate culture truly is (I'm using the term corporate culture to also refer to universities, because it's the same thing).

Even in my teaching career where I branched out to more universities after the first nine years, culture is so evident. Some of the schools I'm affiliated with, have been affiliated with, work so much better than others – partially due to this singular issue of culture.

You may be thinking, as an adjunct, coming in and leaving the building (assuming I know my material and I generally know how to deal with students), why would culture matter?

It really does. Universities are IDENTICAL to corporations in this way. And I have a lot of experience with both, at this point in my career. The students at each school are simply different; they really are.

When I teach an undergrad class, you might think they are essentially the same and when I teach grad courses, you may also think they are similar groups of people.

Students differ, collectively, in each school, from a corporate culture standpoint IN THE EXACT SAME WAY as employees in a company do.

I'm a marketing guy, not a management person, so I'm not going to pretend I'm an expert on this subject (because there are experts and I'd never take away from their expertise and expect the same, mutual respect from them).

But corporate culture is a top-down phenomenon. It comes from the top and filters through the rank-and-file. And once it's set, it's very hard to change. It's changeable but not easy. Culture is also tribal, by the way. I've read many articles where a new CEO in a company comes in from the outside and tries to change the culture – but they're unable to. And often, he or she winds up getting fired in a reasonably short amount of time. To a large extent, due to this, by the way. Not just about perhaps their hard skills not being successful enough to impact the bottom line.

What does this all mean to you when you start your careers? And how do you make sense of it?

I'm going to try my best, based on all my experience and observations over the past 16+ years, to break this down for you in several ways. And while a book unfortunately can't be specific to each person (I know, it sucks, I wish it were different), but I promise this is all related to culture. And I'll try my best to provide you with the guidelines to apply to essentially any job. In some ways, these are questions that you should ask yourself.

One of the first things you should determine as soon as possible (if you can't determine this yet), is whether you're more of a 'large, corporate' person or a 'small, entrepreneurial environment' person.

By the way, you can sometimes also look at this as big fish/small pond or small fish/big pond.

But this is super important – it's so related to corporate culture. Here's why.

It DIRECTLY correlates with your core personality. And you can't change your **core** personality – it's how you're born. And your core personality directly relates to corporate culture.

A large company is going to have a lot more formality, a lot more "official" policy, a lot more bureaucracy (which isn't always a bad word), and a lot more structure.

And maybe I'm a little bias here because I'm more of a large-company person, and while some of the above goes too far in large companies and can get annoying or ridiculous, please remember that large companies NEED to have a much larger degree of policy and structure.

They have more employees and more complex businesses – strategically and operationally. That's the simple truth. Larger companies cannot necessarily make one-off requests for individuals often happen, because they simply can't afford to open too much to interpretation – and implications down the line. Can a large company possibly help just you with a paycheck advance if you're genuinely in a financial emergency? Yes, often HR has special provisions for this type of thing. But you can't, as an employee, supersede the hiring process for interviewing for an internal job – whether it's a lateral or upward move.

A small or smaller company will have either the opposite, or very-much reduced levels of the above.

A second issue that also directly relates is whether you're better suited on the "brand" side or the client/agency side.

When I say "brand" in this context I mean working in-house.

When I say client/agency side, I mean working at an agency-type environment where you have multiple accounts.

This is also super important. Because if you're the type of person that enjoys different personalities and different projects (within your core skill set), then the client/agency side probably works better for you.

If you like an environment where you're using your skill set but you can "dig in your heels" and be committed and have, as I like to say, "skin in the game," then the brand side probably works better for you.

SALESPEOPLE

I sometimes have current and former students contacting me to discuss roles in sales. It happens consistently so I thought it makes sense to at least make this a sub-topic.

I've never been a salesperson. And I don't think I'll ever be.

Now, don't get me wrong, I know we all must "sell" ourselves, but I'm talking about having an official role as a salesperson – that, I've never done.

BUT (yes, once again a BUT, but this time a good one, I hope), I still think I'm qualified to discuss this. I think I'm uniquely qualified. Because in my profession, I deal with salespeople every day. From the other side, as the client that salespeople call on. I don't think there's enough discussed from this side.

I've dealt with and deal with TONS of salespeople. Hundreds, over the years, getting close to the thousand mark.

Can I share with you what I think makes the best and most successful salespeople, if you're considering this as a career path?

By the way, sorry for being judgmental here (I said in the intro I'd stay away from this) but I'm saying this for you...

Everything I'm going to say here is if you're interested in being a GOOD salesperson. A REAL salesperson...one who's committed to sales. For those of you who are hot-shot salespeople, sorry, but this isn't for you.

Because while I've dealt with hundreds of salespeople, I've become genuine, close friends with some of them.

And all the ones I've become friends with are GENUINE. The real McCoy.

Here are the CORE elements of what I think makes a great salesperson. And I'll elaborate, to an extent, on each.

- (Low) Ego. Yes! LOW Ego. Different than confidence. I'll explain.

- Awesome listening skills. Good, genuine salespeople spend 80% of their time LISTENING and only 20% of their time TALKING. The hot shots ruin this by doing the opposite. But I already cursed those people out twice. Real, genuine salespeople LISTEN to their clients.

- Their career PRIORITY is to make MONEY – as MUCH MONEY as possible. And as much as they can (and there's NOTHING wrong with that).

- A general disregard for managing people (and there's also NOTHING wrong with that).

- An exceptional ability to EXECUTE.

- A wonderful memory (on a personal level).

Ego:

We all have an ego but if you're a GOOD salesperson, you need to have an ego that's relatively in-check. I'll explain more right below this with listening skills, because this is all interrelated, but a good salesperson knows when they're in front of clients, it must be about THEM, not you.

Listening Skills:

A good salesperson understands their clients' needs. No, really understands their needs.

In every company I've worked at, the good salespeople know what my needs are as well as the company (and our objectives). Let me give you an example:

Let's say I have a new salesperson who does packaging (outer boxes that you see in the store when you buy something) calls on me and makes an appointment.

The young, inexperienced, hot shots will focus on ONE thing and one thing ONLY: cost. They all claim that they can give me a lower cost than what I'm currently paying.

Some of them might be able to come down in cost, some of them can't. And without getting into why, cost is not even the point.

An experienced, mature, GOOD salesperson will ask me LOTS of questions. And by asking me a lot of questions, they'll come back to me a second time understanding that I'm looking for a host of things: flexible manufacturing, speed, packaging innovation, production quality and reliability – and yes, cost.

See the difference, I hope? This is night and day.

A good salesperson, by asking questions, will understand the totality of my business needs, and might (just might) have a shot at winning some business.

Money and Not Managing People:

I'll combine both because they're very related.

A (career) salesperson has one focus: money. And to make as much as possible.

Now, one thing you should know by now, hopefully, is that I'm not naïve. We all want money – and want to make as much money as possible. Duh, right? But this is different. A career salesperson's MAIN goal is to make money. There's a difference between making as much money as you can AS A BYPRODUCT of what you do for a living vs. money being the GOAL IN AND OF ITSELF.

And since money is the focus, it goes hand-by-hand that an interesting in managing people, building, and managing overall strategy, process, etc., is not a priority.

I know many salespeople who are great at what they do and very effective, and most of them DON'T want the above responsibilities.

Executing:

Another very effective quality of salespeople is that they are close-to-flawless executors. Salespeople don't overthink, and think some more, and then overthink, and think some more. Salespeople DO.

So, if you're more of a "thinker" (in general), sales is probably not for you. If you're more of a doer, then perhaps it is.

Memory:

The best salespeople I know have an incredible memory, especially on a personal level. I know that everyone can benefit from a good memory, but that's not what I mean.

When I say on a personal level (OK, let me admit, I like to tell salespeople things about me, my life, etc.), and the best salespeople will remember so many details. It's incredible. They remember your birthday, various things about your personal friends (what you choose to tell them), they know your favorite food, they know the names of children, they know your choice of beverage, etc.

And whether they just remember this stuff outright, or they go home and take notes when you first tell them things and then memorize it, whatever. It doesn't matter. They are very effective at this.

It makes clients feel special. It just does. And I'm not the type that can be bullshitted to easily, but liking attention is a universal thing that all of us humans crave. Fine, some of us like attention more than others, but we like it when people know things about us. It's just the way it is.

CORPORATE POLITICS

Everyone talks about corporate politics and being politically correct, but since these terms are so overused, many people don't quite know what it's about. There are many standard definitions of politics. But I don't like any that I can find in any dictionary. To me, the definition of politics is quite simple:

Politics is the ability to successfully maneuver within a group dynamic. The ability to influence within a group of people.

So being political means that you can understand situations where people and priorities diverge.

SELF-PROMOTION AND AUDACITY

One of the things you'll need to learn how to do is self-promote, appropriately. Some of you don't need this section – at all. I get that. And you have an advantage.

But most of us need to develop this, to the extent we can.

Self-promotion is not the same as being arrogant. Although, I'll say, you need to have an ego to self-promote. And I don't see any harm in that.
You're going to be responsible for shaping your career. And there will be people who will stand in your way – in subtle as well as overt ways. Some of those things won't be in your control. But self-promotion will always be.

To self-promote, you'll need to feel comfortable to show off your accomplishments as well as your abilities, to the right people – often but not constantly. In other words, you need to learn how to show off without showing off.

Does this make sense? It can be a little hard, I know. But it's important.

To me, self-promotion can come in the form of the following ways:

- Inform
- Remind/Reinforce
- Persuade
- Maintain

To inform is hopefully the most obvious here. Making sure that people around you know the information that you want them to know about you.

Of course, there's a fine line with telling people about you, your work background, skills, etc., and coming across as arrogant. And I wish I could tell you what that precise calibration is, the way a car manufacturer can prescribe what the torque values are on each bolt. But unfortunately, I can't. It's something you'll need to calibrate yourself, in each situation, in each circumstance.

Every now and again, you'll have an opportunity to remind people of, or reinforce your skills. Here's a quick example. I became certified to teach hybrid and distance learning (online) courses in 2016, just as a skillset I wanted to add. I would have never predicted that it would come in handy in the Spring of 2020 when this pandemic called COVID-19 came around.

When the pandemic did hit, and students and instructors needed to immediately shift to online, there was a lot of panic in those early days of March and April of 2020. I reminded the chairs and deans of a few skills that I had experience with online teaching. And for a period of about 9-12 months, I was regarded as a go-to source for advice, help, etc. You need to keep in mind that in March 2020, most instructors didn't even understand the basics of Zoom meetings.

If you're thinking what's the difference between reinforcement and maintenance, reinforcement means you need to remind people what you know. Maintenance means you need to keep it relevant.

To stay relevant, make sure that people, especially newcomers to your organization, in positions of importance, know your skills. Don't assume they do. I'm not suggesting you're not important. But you're not going to be always top-of-mind to most people.

SOFT AND HARD SKILLS

If you haven't already heard these terms, I promise you'll hear them a few times a week – your entire career.

When you begin your career, you'll most likely be hearing them for the first 10 years. And after your first 10 years, you'll likely be saying them and giving younger people the same advice.

SOFT SKILLS

I'll tackle soft skills first, since they are generally regarded as **more important**. This is what helps define you – and your perception with others – to what extent you get along well with others.

But it also does, and manifests itself, in so many other ways. Developing and demonstrating your soft skills will most likely lead to the following:

- A higher level of people trusting you.

- A MUCH better chance of becoming a manager (manager of people).

- A far better chance of being promoted and promoted more often.

- Less chance of being scrutinized or your work being first reviewed for what we all consider "small, mundane" issues.

There are many more positive outcomes, but I don't need to provide you a laundry list. Hopefully the above is enough to get you thinking about its importance.

One of the most important soft skills is the ability to form relationships. These relationships do NOT have to be friendships at work. They simply need to be working relationships. And the ability for others to trust you enough (and refer to the chapter on likability) to be able to offer you information that you need, insight, or possibly even help defend you in certain situations – you'd be surprised! And this relates to what I mean by politics and being political.

Remember, if you want to become a manager, you'll need to prove that you have the skills required to deal with many people and many types of personalities. And all without necessarily becoming emotional on issues.

I once worked for a large company where the President of our division would constantly remind us: stick to the facts! It's good advice that I constantly use.

DON'T GO OVER SOMEONE'S HEAD

One of the worst things you can do is going over someone's head. You've probably heard this before but let me share with you precisely why.

And I must respectfully say, even though more and more younger people feel it's OK to do so, I need to insist that it's not.

This is one of those topics where I'm going to need to ask you to put yourself in that person's shoes.

When you have a legitimate concern or issue, first speak to the person themselves; the first "level," so to speak. When you go over someone's head, you do some, or ALL, of the following:

- You don't allow the person that you have a concern with to answer, and to your surprise, they may have been able to resolve whatever your concern is – or – at least explain why they can't.

- You say something negative about yourself, by showing that you are not mature. And that you don't have enough people skills.

- You expose yourself and others to a change that wasn't necessary.

Notice I'm not even talking about being retaliated against. That's not what this is about, at all.

How would you like it if you did something to someone, inadvertently, and a quick and easy fix would correct it. But you didn't get a chance to do so? Wouldn't you be quite upset?

Are there exceptions? Sure. Such as:

You genuinely tried to resolve the issue professionally but got nowhere. If that happens, then I think you're perfectly in the right to kick it up to the next level.

I need to share an example with you. A few years ago, I started teaching at a university where there's, at times, been a culture of students immediately going to the department chair or dean (for essentially anything). I already had 11 years of teaching experience at that point, but a student had gone to the chair of the department after hearing another student in class use profanity (it wasn't used in a harmful way). I didn't do anything about it since other universities are tolerant, and I also am, to an extent.

I received a very polite and respectful email from the chair mentioning that the culture was a bit different and to simply be mindful of that. And she had innocently asked me how things were, in general. I said in general things were going well and that the take-home mid-term will be next week, etc.

That immediately set something off! She replied, and once again, very politely said that take-home mid-terms (and finals) are not allowed, per school policy. I acknowledged and had to tell all the students that the take-home mid-term would now become an in-class.

Naturally, the students in that class were upset that the mid-term exam was no longer a take-home. Don't get me wrong; many students in that class were great people. But think about the person who went and complained about me being tolerant of someone else cursing and not scolding them; he must have felt pretty stupid for a while.

And you know what? I hope he did feel stupid for a while, hopefully the rest of the semester.

Always try and address the issue with the person you have an issue with, at first. If you can't, or don't feel a level of satisfaction you want, then kick it up a level.

You'll be surprised how many times things will backfire on you when you kick it up before giving the person at the appropriate level a chance to respond, whomever that may be. A colleague, your instructor, etc.

CHAPTER ELEVEN | POLITICIANS AND POLITICS

CHAPTER PURPOSE:
1. Appreciating what elected politics is about.
2. Understanding how highly LIMITED and DISINGENUOUS politicians truly are.

I saved this chapter for one of the last, as to not turn you off. **BEFORE YOU SKIP THIS CHAPTER**, let me say two things:

- Most people wouldn't want to write about politicians and politics. Part of the reason why the United States is in the situation it's in right now is precisely because, for so long, everyone abided by this conventional thinking. And I think it's wrong.

- By reading this chapter, I **promise you'll have a better understanding of politics and you'll be better off**, as a result.

There's a saying which goes something like this:

In politics, if you need to explain something (to your constituents), you've already lost.

That's such a great line. It's insanely accurate and will serve as a part of the backbone for this chapter.

I decided to write this chapter because I think it will genuinely help you make sense out of it all, and when you understand something more, your apprehension tends to go away.

I especially wrote this chapter for people who are so turned off by politics (which I can completely understand why) that they have zero interest, at all.

The one thing I PROMISE you is that I won't talk about politics in a way that's partisan. I assure you.

A lot of you may have heard that all politicians are "liars." I'm not going to argue with that. But don't you feel that's all you've heard/been told, and you want a better understanding why most people talk like this? I want to try and break it down for you, in hopefully a more meaningful AND useful way.

When I was an undergrad, I think I spent almost my entire college experience walking around with a peace sign around my neck. I don't regret it one bit.

I'm sharing this is because I was, and perhaps you are too, very idealistic. No, I mean I was super idealistic. And it felt great! It's a very normal thing for young people to feel that way.

I used to believe in certain politicians and what they said. I would hang on almost every word – and be all in!

Now that I'm older, I'm a little less idealistic and more pragmatic (also a very normal thing as you get older), and I now have a completely different view on politicians. And want to share with you what no one shared with me. And believe me, you'll be better off for it.

The business of politics is just that – a business. It's a politician's career. You're probably thinking you already know this, but it gets worse.

It is NOT the role of a politician to teach you ANYTHING!

Nor is it the role of a politician to HELP you in any way!

The role of a politician is to get a good, baseline sense of your emotions and exploit and run with it.

That's all it is folks; all it is.

I've thought about this a lot. And when a politician does do good on a promise, and it benefits you, I can honestly say that the best way to treat those situations is to see them as a fortunate consequence, that happened to work in your general favor. Notice I'm using the word consequence, as opposed to "fulfilling a campaign promise."

If a politician makes good on a campaign promise and it benefits you, it's because it first benefitted them and their interests. You came second. (Hell, maybe even third).

The reason why I'm using the word consequence is because a politician's priority is not to do work on things that they said on the campaign trail.

A politician's number 1 priority is to get elected and then re-elected.

Remember guys, it's a business. It's their job. You know how you have your job, because when you show up and do certain things, hopefully every two weeks or on the 15th and last day of the month you get paid?

They're doing the same exact thing you are.

Ever notice that you can be a former politician, but no one really calls it an unemployed politician. You can be an unemployed engineer, or marketing manager, looking for your next role. Because that implies you have skills in something concrete. But there's a reason why we don't have a term called unemployed politician – because aside from getting elected, making tons of phone calls every week, and raising money – there's not much to the job.

A politician is not interested in your thoughts or opinions. They are only interested in how you **feel**.

And if you, in general, represent their base, how you feel is what they'll tell you how they feel.

Don't have a job? Great! Mr. or Ms. Politician will tell you how their economic policies will get you one.

Have a job? Great! Mr. or Ms. Politician will tell you how their party was responsible for getting you the good job you have. And their economic policies will allow you to keep the job you like.

Mr. or Ms. Politician will tell you how their economic policies will get you the job you want AND deserve.

Isn't that real sweet of them? Like a family member or close friend, they'll come across as though they know you and tell you that you deserve the type of job you want. What saints, these politicians are. (That's sarcasm, folks, but hopefully you picked up on that).

If the politician's party is the opposition, they prefer that you don't have a job. You'll be angrier that way – and more likely to vote for them.

The party in power wants you to be happy! The opposition party wants you to be mad as hell!

But right or wrong, anger will always be a stronger emotion than happiness. When you're happy, you're more likely to be content. And therefore, happiness is a lot more passive, right?

When you're angry, you tend to be a lot more active! And you want to see something different done.

This is tribalism. Tribes demand loyalty, and in return they offer the sense of security and belonging.

Tribes are not about ideology or beliefs.

I'm not a scholar, and there have been many well-researched articles on this and even a few good books, but in case you don't know, tribalism is on the rise.

If you believe in equal rights for the LGBTQ+ community, are pro-choice, believe that climate change is a real threat, etc., they do too.

If you believe in marriage as a union between a man and a woman, are pro-life, not sure that climate change is real, or humans cannot change its course, they do too.

The beauty of all of this is that there's a politician to fit your perspective.

Wow, look at that! Works like magic!

It's not magic. You know what it is? Formulaic.

Sometimes I think that all politicians are like fortune cookies. You know that little slip of paper in the cookie?

They all have general messages that seem to always fit your mood, in some way. I know, we call them talking points. Hmm...interesting. Coincidence? Umm, no. Those are written the way they are, by design.

Another thing that's important to share is that I IMPLORE you, for your own sake, to not get angry at politicians. They are NOT worth you getting angry over.

OK, so I'm still young enough to say this...

You know how many dads in the world seem to get angry at politicians they don't like and yell and curse at the TV? I know some moms also do this, but let's admit it, it's mainly dads.

Don't do that! You're wasting your time and your energy.

I know it can be hard, and I've also done it in the past, but over the past few years I've grown here and made a lot of progress. And you can, too.

Trust me:
Donald Trump, Barack Obama, George W. Bush, and Bill Clinton **DON'T GIVE A GODDAMN ABOUT YOU (OR ME)**, as individuals.

I said I wouldn't be partisan in this chapter – and this isn't partisan. I think it's probably safe to say (probably) that many young people in the United States have a positive impression of Barack Obama, yes? I think that's a fair statement. But TRUST me on this...let's say that the fate of the presidential election rested in your hands, and Obama and his team knew this, but they also knew you'll be voting democrat.

And let's say you needed to go vote, but your dear sweet grandmother was in the hospital, and you needed to visit her the same day as election day. Barack Obama would want a status report from his aides, and his team tells him that you also needed to visit your grandmother in the hospital. Do you want to know what Obama would ask his aides? "Well, did s/he put in their vote before visiting the old hag?"

I am NOT calling your sweet, dear little old grandmother a hag (I'm sure she's a fine lady)...but my point is that there's a good chance Obama would. Folks, he's a politician. He doesn't CARE about us at all! (None of them do).

They never have, never will. So, stop caring about them. When you utilize your energy, whether it's by yourself or with friends, speaking in an angry way about politicians, you're wasting your time.

If you're having a discussion on politics in terms of issues and how it affects you, and the positions of politicians, that's TOTALLY fine. That's different.

But having a discussion (or argument if there's disagreement) about the politicians on a personal level is absurd.

Don't you see the folly and foolishness about getting your head all wrapped into this?

Politicians love when you hate their opponent. You're doing so much of the work for them! They're getting FREE advertising. And what do you get? Heartache? A possible argument or even a physical fight that wasn't necessary?

Politicians only get nervous when you do something they do NOT want you to do, at all, under ANY circumstances:

THINK.

If you did some 'moronic' thing such as thinking, they would need to completely change their strategy. Remember my chapter on likability.

If you think, you're really disrupting the political world order. And you're challenging the power structure. They don't want that.

And when it comes to a presidential candidate, think for a moment what happens once they win their respective party's nomination. They then look for a running mate.

In "management 101," we learn that a good manager hires people that are smarter than they are, as you know. Business leaders say that so much that what was once good advice has become a cliché, unfortunately. Nonetheless, do you think a presidential candidate looks for a running mate that is:

- Smarter than them?

- Makes up for their own weaknesses, in terms of actual skills?

- A policy wonk?

- Complements their style?

- Someone they'll be able to easily work with?

Nope! Sorry. The running mate will be selected based on whether that person will help the nominee WIN the election. (And re-election).

You're only as good as your vote.

And you're either a voter for that politician, or you're not. That's all.

So next time you vote, next time it's election season, please, don't get your "panties in a bunch."

Understand how incredibly limited they are to your life, for the most part.

CHAPTER TWELVE | NUANCE

CHAPTER PURPOSE:
- Understanding how nuance can genuinely be a competitive advantage in your life.

This chapter isn't particularly long but I wanted to make nuance one of the life principles in this book because it's incredibly strong yet undervalued.

Nuance is stronger than you may think because it can directly translate into a competitive advantage, in various aspects of your life.

Nuance is rare and not easy to replicate.

Nuance is important because it ultimately boils down to one reason: it has an incredible way of making you stand out from everyone else.

Let me give you my definition of nuance, from a social context, before going any further:

Nuance is about doing things that may seem 'small' but have tremendous meaning. Nuance means giving a damn.

I promise, I'll explain.

If you can embrace and practice nuance in your life, people WILL notice. Not everyone will notice, granted. But enough people will. And the RIGHT people will. The smart people, the good people, the caring people. They're the ones who will notice.

I'm not here to give you an English lesson, but some may see the word 'subtlety' as a synonym for nuance. Subtlety is something different. That has more to do with 'softness.'

I mean nuance, in a sociological sense. Nuance doesn't necessarily have to be soft. It can, but what I mean by nuance is the EXTRA. Going the extra mile, or the 'finishing touches.' That's nuance.

But must be genuine. It can't be provoked into action by ANY external factors. It's internal. Nuance responds to the external world by how you act. But it can't be motivated by any external factors, such as social convention, someone asking you to do something, a trend, something that's a cultural phenomenon, etc. Those are NOT nuance.

Nuance also needs to be completely unexpected. That's part of why it's very genuine.

Also, it can't be part of your social repertoire. Nuance doesn't come from your mind. It comes from your heart, soul, and spirit.

Nuance comes from your **character** - not your personality.

No offense salespeople: you don't get credit here and can't take any ownership of nuance. Your sales training and "sales voice" are fine in terms of your personality – whether real or manufactured for your career. But it's not nuance.

Let me provide some examples of nuance, in its true form.

Example 1:

Recently, I taught a senior-level Capstone course that had an actual client project component to it. Long story short, at the end of the semester, the clients come in for a presentation lead by the assigned student teams.

One client, a CEO who is a very busy person, jotted down all five of the group's names when they introduced themselves. When it was time for him to ask questions at the end of the presentation, he knew each student's name.

That evening, I emailed the entire class asking if they noticed that.

Do you know what a long way that goes? To have someone at a high level, who is effectively a stranger and the first time you're meeting them, to remember who you are and call you by your first name?

What does that show? That shows that he cared and is a genuine leader. In plain English, it showed that he **gave a damn**.

Example 2:

My favorite teacher is a professor in the sociology department at NYU, when I was an undergrad. And she displayed nuance a very long time ago –

something that I've never forgotten in over 20 years and have used myself from time-to-time.

When I went through a difficult period in my life (after graduating and entering law school for a brief period before deciding to quit and pursue an MBA), I went back to my professor's office unannounced to get her advice, and needed her to console me, etc.

When she saw me knock on her door, she knew something was wrong. She told me to come in and sit down, got out of her chair, and sat next to me in one of her guest chairs on the other side of her desk.

Why did she do that? To this day (and I keep in touch with her), she never told me, and I never asked. I didn't need to ask.

She did that because she knew I needed her help, and by sitting next to me she was able to be more supportive and more like a peer, with her body language. As opposed to sitting behind her desk which is more authoritarian. It made me feel more at ease.

Once again, she showed that she **gave a damn**. That's nuance.

Example 3:

This hasn't happened too often over the years but now and again I'll have a student drop my class. And they'll send me an email – or make sure they bump into me – and they'll let me know why they dropped the class, and it didn't have anything to do with me. And some will go even further and thank me and tell me that they hope they can take it with me another semester.

Wow, that's someone with a lot of **character** – and a hell of a lot of **class**.

While this will be easier for some than others, everyone can learn how to incorporate some elements of nuance – and as I said, this WILL make a difference.

On the other end of nuance is what others who can do things for you will notice...the small things, from you.

Don't take this lightly. Sometimes the small things that people notice about you will be the deciding factor in whether you get a job or some type of opportunity. Selected on a committee, etc. When someone says "there's something about that person" referring to you, this is sometimes due to nuance.

I'm not talking superficial things like holding a door open or a pulling out a chair for someone. Or saying thank you. Those are nice too, in their own right. But that's not nuance, really. That's being polite.

I'm talking about making sure you don't have your back to someone while speaking to them. That goes a long way.

I'm talking about when one person sends an entire team an email and asks for a quick confirmation on let's say a time/day for a meeting. And most people not only reply to all with something like "works for me." And you just reply to the sender and write "yes." A smart person will give you credit for that, believe me. They'll notice you're one of the few who didn't reply to all. And "yes" is 2/3rds less words than "works for me."

I'm talking about calling someone and leaving an unexpected voicemail thanking them for something that no one else would even think of thanking them for.

Nuance, if properly understood and embraced, can really set you apart from others.

Embrace it, and you'll get paid back at various times in your life.

CONCLUSION

Sigmund Freud essentially spent his entire adult life talking about what was wrong with people and humanity.

Towards the end of his life, when he was pretty old and he, as well as close friends knew he wasn't going to be around much longer, someone asked Freud if there was anything decent...anything good about humanity.

Freud had a very simple answer.

He said: Sure. The ability to love and be loved. And the ability to do work that you care about.

And now...I wish those two things for you.

I hope you saw one overarching theme in this book: to THINK.

All I've EVER wanted the world to do is THINK.

I don't care what your IQ or EQ is. We may be at different levels, but we can ALL raise the bar of our thinking, and our thought process.

If everyone engaged in genuine thinking, this place called earth would be so much better. I promise you, promise you, promise you. Did I promise you?

One last nugget of wisdom from my hero George Carlin. He said the biggest problem with humans is that we have squandered the greatest gift that we were given: thinking.

In the Acknowledgments, I ended with a thank you.

Please do your very best thinking in this world we all live in.

And one more time...thank you.

That's all I want to say. That's all I've ever wanted to say.

BONUS CHAPTER: CHAPTER FIVE FROM MY PRESENTATION SKILLS BOOK

I wanted to add one full chapter from my presentation skills book: It's Called Presenting, Not Talking Out Loud. A Quick, Strategic Guide For Effective Presentations

OK, so I'm embedding an entire chapter from one book into another in the hopes of selling more books.

So, what's my crime? A guy can't try and sell a few books? ☺. I was honest throughout this entire book, so I'm being honest here, too.

CHAPTER FIVE | OBJECTIVE

As mentioned earlier, you will want to establish what your overall objective is when preparing your presentation. In simple terms, always ask yourself what is it that you're trying to *achieve*. While this may seem a bit obvious, it's sometimes taken for granted.

Are you trying to share some information with an audience? If so, it is probably more than an FYI. If it *is* just a simple FYI, and you'd rather discuss it rather than sending an email, then we probably don't even need to call those situations "presentations."

If you're sharing information, such as an update, are you also trying to persuade? You may not be selling them, per se, but are you trying to influence some type of behavior i.e. offering an alternative insurance plan or unveiling a new business strategy that requires employees to embrace a new mindset? Alternatively, are you doing a highly interactive type of presentation that requires high audience involvement?

SHOW AND TELL

Remember when you were a kid and had "show and tell" in school? Those were exciting – and simpler – times, for sure. And I'm assuming that your kindergarten or first-grade teacher didn't grill you on your objective when you came to show and tell, right?

But if you really think about it, even the simple, innocent activity of show and tell can begin to teach us how we should think of presentations, as adults.

I'm sure you brought something into class to discuss? Maybe it was a new doll that you were excited about. Maybe you didn't have a toy to bring but you brought pictures from a family vacation, and you told all your cute, little classmates about it? Maybe you got a new puppy and while you couldn't bring Fido to school, you decided to tell the students why you got a dog instead of a cat, because of your allergies, etc.

Anyway, the innocence of kids, coupled with show and tell and all its unassuming objectives can give us a pretty good starting point to think about your presentation.

THE FOUR OBJECTIVES

There are generally four main objectives of a presentation (many authors will use different names), but they essentially boil down to the same four. And they are not always fixed-point. In other words, sometimes you can do a presentation that has a bit of a blend of two or more.

For example, if you're a coach giving your players a locker room pep talk on what they need to do to win, don't necessarily assume this is a tell/sell situation just because you're the coach and the players are your subordinates. This could be both tell/sell and consult/join, since a good coach knows that he needs the support from the players (the audience) to carry out the mission. Lecturing players simply isn't going to cut it. I use Al Pacino's "locker room" speech from *Any Given Sunday* to illustrate this (see appendix B).

Borrowing a page from Mary Munter and Lynn Hamilton, the objective of a presentation can be thought of as one of the following:

- Tell/Sell – used primarily when you want the audience to learn from you.

- Consult/Join – used primarily when you want to learn from the audience, or need buy-in.

You can categorize them in many ways, such as:

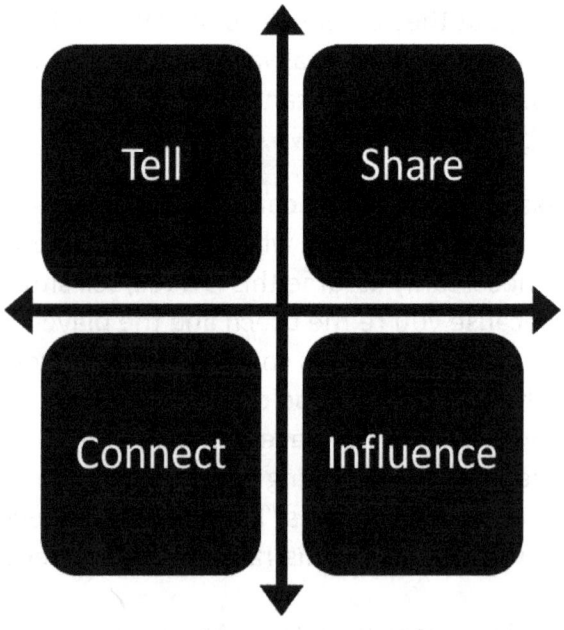

Let's map this out a little more specifically so you can get a better appreciation of what skills and attributes go with these, and hopefully you'll get a better handle on how to prepare your presentation.

	Skills	Attributes
Tell	Present Simplify Summarize Interpret	Clarity Precision Discipline Confidence Tenacity
Connect	Listen Question Discuss Probe Debate Provide/Receive Feedback	Openness Candor Patience Curiosity Humility Accessibility
Share	Engage Collaborate Facilitate Navigate	Respect Trust Empathy Self-awareness
Influence	Propose Persuade Lead	Transparency Authenticity/Passion Decisiveness

Another important issue when forming your objective is to ensure your presentation isn't too broad. We'll discuss agendas in another chapter but, as you begin to structure your presentation based on what you hope to achieve, make sure the various components are not so general that they become separate presentations in of themselves.

In other words, try not to do too much and be overly ambitious. Presentations and speeches can land you a promotion, a new job, a new account. Heck, a solid presentation/speech sometimes changes the world in some way (see Nelson Mandela). However, they are specific in terms of their objective. People who understand strategy know that by staying focused, they stay relevant.

PLAN, BUT WITH A LITTLE FLEXIBILITY

If you plan *too* 'well' in advance, you may come across as too scripted and inauthentic, so avoid doing this. You don't want to be perceived as a "cookie cutter" or "plain vanilla" speaker. Plan well but leave in a little "wiggle room." It is understandable if in your line of work you mainly deliver tell/sell presentations that are generally straightforward. Add your own flair and dynamic, though, and make something that might be boring a little *less* boring. If you plan well but are perceived as "militant" about it, you'll quickly gain the reputation being a boring and rigid presenter.

We all know what happens when you grab a handful of sand too tightly. It slides through your fingers. If you hold it too loosely, it falls from the sides of your hands. Hold it just right, with a little firmness, and most of the sand can stay in your hand.

LEVEL OF DETAILS

The most important thing here is to make sure you don't confuse detail with simplification. To the extent you can, be sure to simplify when and where it makes sense. Simplification is universally good, since it means you're making your content easy to digest.

The number of details you provide partly has to do with your depth of knowledge of the subject. And as you hopefully guessed by now, after reading everything I said about audiences – it's also about your audience.

When I took business communications during my MBA studies, the instructor mentioned that good/the best presenters have a strong command of details. That's good advice, but I've changed my opinion about that advice over the years. It doesn't necessarily mean that you need to share all the details. Keep that in mind.

Knowing the number of details to provide can be tricky but understanding your audience and your objective should make this a lot less daunting. I touched on this above with the example on heart surgeons but let's expand a bit more.

We have a tendency, especially when we're passionate about our subject, to give far too much detail than necessary. It's a natural inclination, and I think we do it for the following reasons:

1. We're presenting to a group of superiors, and we feel that we are proving our value by showcasing our command of the details.

Most of us, myself included, have been in this situation. Have some faith in your superiors and don't overcompensate. They themselves were once in your position, but even if they weren't, they trust you. Don't waste their time. If they need more detail, they will ask.

2. We think we need to demonstrate how we reached a conclusion.

This is different than connecting the dots, as I mentioned with the previous heart surgeon example. Here, we feel as though we need to justify our conclusions, approach, recommendations, etc. by offering the logic or sequence of events that got us there. You don't always need to. In business, we primarily care about results!

3. We assume that since *we* care so much about the subject matter, our *audience* also does.

This is a classic mistake. Sorry to say this, but even people who are interested in the presentation simply may not care as much about the subject as we do. I know this can be a bit disconcerting because we want people to care. But it's better that this come from me rather than being unsuccessful with your presentation and then *really* being upset.

So how do we know what is the right number of details?

My best advice is think about when you should *stop*. In other words, consider when you've made your point to your audience. At what point do you no longer need to share additional information to support each major idea? Stop there. Another way to approach this is to ask yourself, "at what point does the amount of detail I share stop adding value to the audience?"

Providing too many details can have the reverse effect of what you hoped for. I have a lot of respect for R&D people and have worked with them and other technical people throughout my career. But sometimes technical people make the mistake of offering too much detail to non-technical audiences. In those cases, it's not only that the number of details offered is unnecessary, but there's a good chance the audience, often merchants and marketing people, won't understand it. So be mindful of this.

Think for a moment about a recent vacation you went on. You've returned and are telling your friends and co-workers about your trip. You may give certain friends more detail than co-workers, but you'll still leave out the things that have no bearing on anything, right?

Having a time limit for your presentation can also help keep you guided.

Here's an example:

You're doing a presentation to a general audience on the 4-stroke engine, commonly known as the gasoline-powered engine. A four-stroke, or four-cycle, engine is an internal combustion (IC) engine in which the piston completes four separate strokes while turning the crankshaft.

Look at the difference between the original and condensed version.

I'll just use the first stroke as opposed to all four (original version from Wikipedia):

> **ORIGINAL:** 1.Intake: also known as induction or suction. This stroke of the piston begins at top dead center (T.D.C.) and ends at bottom dead center (B.D.C.). In this stroke, the intake valve must be in the open position while the piston pulls an air-fuel mixture into the cylinder by producing vacuum pressure into the cylinder through its downward motion. The piston is moving down as air is being sucked in by the downward motion against the piston.

> **CONDENSED:** 1.Intake: This stroke of the piston begins at the top and ends at the bottom. The piston is moving down as air is being sucked in.

Hopefully you notice that in the condensed version, the nature of the information hasn't changed. I just reduced the *amount* of information.

Another red flag that you might be offering too much detail is if your presentation's topic fundamentally changes at some point during your delivery – literally.

I once observed a presentation that had a lot of great elements to it in the beginning but quickly derailed. The topic was on immigration and the presentation started out very strong. The presenter began by discussing the crisis in Syria – but soon enough the presentation shifted from immigration to the Syrian war.

It wasn't intentional, but the entire presentation changed because the presenter got wrapped up in too many details on the war.

I made a video on my YouTube channel that you can check out, called "Talk Too Much? Here's Some Advice That Helped Me!"

What I discuss in that video is that while it might be hard to somewhat accept at first, not everyone cares about a particular subject as much as we do. Sometimes people won't care about a subject that we do at all. But even those that are interested in the same topic may not be as "passionate" as we are.

So, as I said in Chapter One in this book, on the last "C" – Context. It's important to understand how much information our audience, whether an audience of 1 or 100, is willing to absorb – and needs to absorb.

Check out that video when you get a chance; I hope it helps.

BONUS CHAPTER: MOST THINGS ARE AN 'INSIDE JOB'

I wanted to include a chapter on how most people, who do things that are not necessarily legal or ethical, get caught. The purpose of this quick bonus chapter isn't to show you how to not get caught. Instead, I hope the value here is understanding relationships.

When you examine things that fall within the nature of the above, you'll notice that often times what brings someone down boils down to a whistleblower, perhaps. Or if not a whistleblower, sometimes just a disgruntled person who was on the inside and didn't get what they felt they deserved, on some level.

For example, there was the infamous Pamela Anderson and Tommy Lee sex tape, that went around like wildfire in the late 1990s. I'm using the word 'tape' because it was a tape – this was prior to streaming. The internet was still kind of new'ish, and the explicit tape was clandestinely made available for sale.

How did that tape leak? It turns out all of this happened because Tommy Lee and Pamela Anderson were doing renovations to their California mansion. And Tommy Lee decided to not pay the contractor doing the work in full and fired him. The contractor found the tape amongst other things he stole to make his financial loss whole. And that's how it all started.

On a completely different topic (and this is local), there's a fairly large, important town in north Jersey not far from where I grew up, Secaucus.

There was an article that came out in December, 2021 where the local go-go bar in Secaucus, NJ was raided by the police for a drug sting. The chief of police, Dennis Miller, was quoted as saying, 'The Secaucus Police Department will continue to investigate every complaint from our citizenry.'

I made a YouTube video on this called 'Cocaine, Strip Clubs, and Prostitutes: The Way The World Really Works.'

I'm a guy who is pro-police. But the truth is that the police chief wasn't lying but being disingenuous.

If you look at that quote, your average citizen isn't going to make a complaint about drugs in a go-go bar. How and why would they even know about it?

While I don't know for certain, I can tell you how this prostitution raid and drug bust originated from. It was either a disgruntled customer (regular), or a disgruntled/former dancer, bartender, or bouncer. That's how these things come about in the real world, folks.

BONUS CHAPTER: HOW TO ADMIRE YOUR HEROES THE RIGHT WAY

Hopefully, you have heroes that you admire. Maybe you have several. And that's great.

However, there's one thing about heroes that most people don't seem to understand, which is the point of having a hero in the first place.

Too many people put their heroes, whether they're living or dead, on pedestals that are so high, there's no possible way to reach them.

The purpose of having heroes is not to be in sheer awe of them. Sure, admire your heroes; I do mine. But the purpose of a hero is to STUDY them, LEARN, and be INSPIRED.

You (and me) will probably never achieve the level of greatness that our heroes have. **But that's OK, it's not necessary**. By admiring your heroes in a healthy way, you'll get as close as possible – and that's genuinely what it's about!

Let me use an example: many people consider Nelson Mandela, the first black president of South Africa and the end of apartheid, as their hero. Fine. No, more than fine. Great.

But too many people walk around saying the following words. Wow, he was a saint. Can you believe he spent 27 years in prison and still achieved what he did? What a saint!

Nelson Mandela was NOT a saint. He was a person who achieved a tremendous amount, but made of flesh and blood, just like you.

My understanding is that Mandela was keenly aware of this during his life. And he went as far as saying:

I am not a saint. Unless you consider a saint, a sinner who keeps on trying.

Mohandas Gandhi (by the way, please don't call him Mahatma Gandhi or the Mahatma, it drives me crazy, and that wasn't his name) was also aware of his star power and rock star status. In his autobiography, Gandhi said:

Everyone wants to adorn my pictures. But no one wants to take my advice.

There's a reason why we call heroes, heroes. They are rare and hard to imitate. God only made one Gandhi, one Mandela, one Socrates, etc.

There are no duplicate copies available. But that's OK. Don't try and emulate your heroes or simply worship them on paper. Have them inspire you.

Have them cause you to go through pain and suffering as you proceed in fulfilling your mission.

And if you can do that, you understand the value of heroes and how to utilize them.

BONUS CHAPTER: WHEN YOU'RE LOOKING FOR STEAK, DON'T SETTLE FOR HAMBURGER

Vegetarians, vegans, and maybe other groups who don't eat meat, my apologies. I'm not here to offend you. Change the metaphor if that helps.

I've learned throughout the years to not settle on things that you didn't plan on. These are "second best" solutions that may seem close enough to your original goal, but they are miles apart.

A quick, prominent example, to start.

I'm not a big sports person but I remember in 2007, Yankees famed general manager, Joe Torre, was getting close to the end of his relationship with the Yankees after a series of losses. After the 2007 season, the Yankees offered Torre a nonnegotiable contract of one year for a base salary of $5 million and an additional $1 million bonus based on winning several benchmarks.

Joe Torre considered the offer, which was only for one year, and a salary cut, as an insult and turned down the offer.

And while I can only speak in generalities, sometimes an offer is a real offer, but it's really a "hey, we don't hate you but also don't really like you so here's a lousy offer that we hope you turn down anyway."

And if you think about an offer like that, it's in the company's best interests and has very little to do with you.

One of the key things to learn here is to engage in things and be around people and organizations that WANT you. Just because you may be offered a job (and I know how important that is), these types of offers are heavily lopsided. And they are almost entirely focused on the benefits of the organization. (Yes, all companies will engineer everything in their favor, but most times they do consider the individual, to an extent). Not in these cases.

Unless you're in dire straits or have hit rock bottom, don't settle for things that you don't want in the first place. You'll be unhappy, you'll fail, and most likely that will serve as a justification by the company that you weren't all that good in the first place.

In case you're thinking about United States vice presidents that first ran for president, well, you're on to something.

Of all recent history, how many US vice presidents go on to get the presidency after their bosses' term is up? Not many.

I once had a job interview at a very large, prominent retail supermarket chain for a corporate role as Director of Sourcing. I was about 29 or so, at the time, and although I had enough on my resume and cover letter to get me the interview, when I interviewed, the company felt I wasn't "quite there" yet for a director role. They felt I would get there, but I wasn't there – yet.

They liked my candidacy and instead offered me a job as sourcing manager. It would have also been a good role, with a solid salary (obviously not as high as the director role) and the hope would be that I'd eventually fill into the director role in a few years.

And I needed a job at the time; I didn't have a current one. But when human resources offered me this alternative position, I politely turned it down.

Some may think this is a dumb move. And to those who may feel that way, I understand and I'm not in opposition with you. I'm sure I make many dumb moves on a weekly basis, then and now.

But I made the difficult but important decision and didn't regret it (that was around 15 years ago, so I no longer care), but nonetheless, I didn't regret it.

The sourcing manager role was to report to the director role. In other words, if I got the director job, I would supervise others. Now I'd be the one who was supervised by whomever the director would eventually be.

If I took that sourcing manager role, and even if it would have turned out to something more in a few years, the truth is I would have been unhappy as a sourcing manager on my first day on the job.

Who the hell wants to start a new job unhappy at a large, well-known company starting on day 1?

I mean, sometimes we start a new job unhappy on day 1, but that's when we already know it's a shitty job, from the start.

I'm not a human resources expert (but I've been around companies long enough), and something tells me that companies don't offer these alternative scenarios nearly as much as they used to. I think they've understood the "messiness" it usually creates.

My sense is that human resources also is better at understanding that these "alternatives" are disingenuous.

Nevertheless, whether it's an offer for a different job that you don't really want, or some other type of offer in your life, unless you're in dire straits, don't take it.

Wait a bit, the steak is still thawing. The hamburger is OK but just a hamburger.

BIBLIOGRAPHY

This bibliography is by no means comprehensive. It's designed to be selective, and hopefully provide credit where its due. Much of this guide comes from my scratch notes and not formal research. Since the flavor of this guide has always been casual, the bibliography is also reflective of that.

1958, Public Papers of the Presidents of the United States, Dwight D. Eisenhower, 1957, Containing the Public Messages, Speeches, and Statements of the President, Remarks at the National Defense Executive Reserve Conference, Date: November 14, 1957, Start Page 817, Quote Page 818, Published by the Federal Register Division, National Archives and Records Service, General Services Administration, Washington D.C.

1988 February 1, Esquire, Volume 109, Number 2, The Sporting Life: The Brawling Existentialist by Mike Lupica (Columnist for New York Daily News), Start Page 55, Quote Page 57, Published by Esquire Associates, New York. (Classic Esquire Archive Online; accessed August 25, 2021)

Carson, Johnny. (1986). George Carlin Interview. Retrieved from https://youtu.be/5xCDlzAsFAM

Carlin, George. (2012). George Calin Interview. Retrieved from https://youtu.be/CewUVZZMXT8

Gandhi, Mohandas Karamchand. *Gandhi: An Autobiography: The Story Of My Experiments With Truth.* Beacon Press, 1993

The Marshmallow Challenge: https://www.marshmallowchallenge.com

Munter, Mary, and Lynn Hamilton. *Guide to Managerial Communication: Effective Business Writing and Speaking.* New Jersey: Pearson, 2013

Pacino, Al. (2016). New York Film Academy Interview. Retrieved from https://youtu.be/T44hIXaHbHo

Wikipedia contributors, "Internal combustion engine," *Wikipedia, The Free Encyclopedia,* https://en.wikipedia.org/w/index.php?title=Internal_combustion_engine&oldid=857304606 (accessed June 26, 2018).

Al Golzari is a senior-level consumer product professional with 20+ years' experience in product development, innovation, sourcing, and vendor management along with 15+ years of adjunct teaching experience at all levels, including executive MBA. He has worked at various companies including LBrands, Target, and Macy's, along with consulting work.

A native of northern New Jersey, he currently resides in New York City.

www.ingramcontent.com/pod-product-compliance
Lightning Source LLC
Chambersburg PA
CBHW060747050426
42449CB00008B/1311